MOTHER

ALSO BY MARY MOTLEY KALERGIS

Giving Birth (1983)

MOTHER

A Collective Portrait by Mary Motley Kalergis

E. P. DUTTON  NEW YORK

Published in the United States by E. P. Dutton, a division of NAL Penguin
Inc., 2 Park Avenue, New York, N.Y. 10016.

Published simultaneously in Canada by
Fitzhenry and Whiteside Limited, Toronto.

Library of Congress Cataloging-in-Publication Data
Mother : a collective portrait.
1. Mothers—United States—Interviews. 2. Motherhood—
United States. I. Kalergis, Mary Motley.
HQ759.M873 1987   306.8'743   86-29187
ISBN: 0-525-24525-1

COBE

Designed by Nancy Etheredge

10 9 8 7 6 5 4 3 2 1

First Edition

To my husband, David,
and our sons,
Pie, Hugh, and David, Jr.

ACKNOWLEDGMENTS

Much appreciation and gratitude goes to my assistant, Kathy Bowers; my editor, Meg Blackstone; my agent, Susan Protter; and all the admirable women in this book. I thank each of you for collaborating with me on this project.

PREFACE

This collection of photographs and interviews is a group portrait of contemporary American motherhood. The book follows a woman's relationship with the role of mother from pregnancy to the time her children have children. It explores how women's individual lives are affected by the responsibility of nurturing a child and how their individual circumstances and dispositions influence their mothering. The mother of an infant or young child has a very different perspective from the mother of teenagers or a grandmother. A new mother has to struggle with a whole new identity while the mother of older children has to learn to accept her children as teenagers and then as adults. Once her children have left the house and have had children of their own, a grandmother may have the opportunity to be reflective. Although the relationship changes over the years, it never completely ends.

In a time when a woman's role inside and outside the home often determines whether she is considered a "good mother" or a "bad mother," I've attempted to put aside these judgments and respectfully observe the unique circumstances of each of these women, each of these mothers. A poor, single mother's definition of good mothering might be steady employment, which will allow her to put meals on her child's table. A middle-class woman, with a husband who can support them all, might decide that staying home with her children is the most valuable job she could have, while a feminist might have a career to show her children that mothers as well as fathers need to have power in the marketplace.

The procreative urge and its repercussions cross economic, racial, and religious differences. A woman's place and time in history have a tremendous influence over the number of choices she can make in her life. It's my hope that this book will enable people to appreciate the complexities involved in the title of Mother, a role that is often considered merely instinctual.

MOTHER

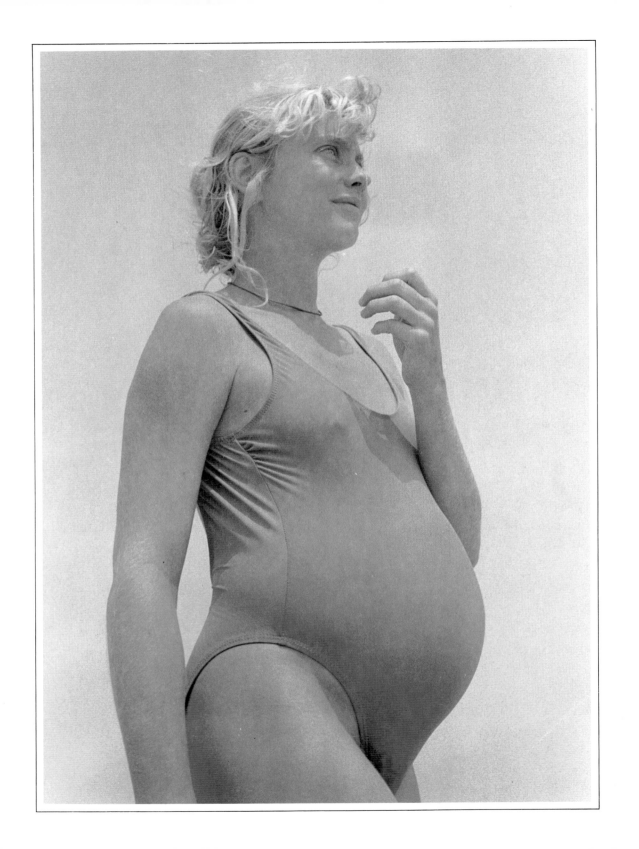

Last summer I was told I was sterile and would never have children. I had PID from a Dalkon Shield IUD and was involved in a lawsuit when I got pregnant. What a surprise! I was reading a lot of articles on in vitro fertilization and adoption when I conceived. I was sure I had an ectopic pregnancy. I was sick from morning to night for the first five months. I was nauseated and exhausted all the time. I missed the feeling of being athletic. It was more like a disease than a baby until my pregnancy began to show and I could feel [the baby] move inside of me.

I work free-lance as a fabric designer and it takes a lot of drive and motivation to keep working. I have been so inward feeling and unmotivated that I've feared all my creative muses and ambition have forsaken me forever. I feel more passive, more traditionally feminine. I'm much more aware of my dreams lately. I dreamed I found a little baby on the street, almost frozen. I rushed it to the hospital, but they said the baby was already dead. I couldn't accept that so I began to breathe into its mouth. Immediately the child warmed up and opened his eyes. I woke up realizing I still was in touch with my own creative powers. Ever since then I've felt less lost in my pregnancy.

I don't want any pain medication while giving birth because it seems like one of the quintessential experiences of being a woman, of being alive and human—to have a child. I don't want my senses dulled at that time. I've always made a conscious effort not to avoid things, no matter how difficult they might be.

I wish I had more role models of women who have children and are able to continue their work. My own mother stopped being a nurse when she had her kids and my sister gave up teaching when she had children. I'm afraid of losing my work in design, which means a lot to me. I'm uncomfortable with the idea of paying a woman to care for my child while I work because I'm not used to it. I guess I'm going to have to get used to it. I have to learn a whole new way to be.

I admire my sister for having the guts to say "I've got my own power and respect. I don't need to work for anyone." Her job is raising her children. After years of graduate school and working, it's hard to imagine my identity will be able to change that much after I become a mother, but only time will tell. Somebody asked my midwife what it was really like to have a child. She walked over to the sofa where the couple was sitting and sat right on top of them so they couldn't move. I'm the first person of all my friends to have a child. I realize I'm moving into a great unknown.

3

My first three months of pregnancy were unreal to me—I couldn't take in the reality that I was going to be a mother. I think we need at least nine months to prepare for that change in our lives. I loved to feel the baby move inside me. It reassured me that it was really alive. The last few weeks of waiting for the birth were intense. The uncertainty of when I'd hold my child in my arms and see his little face overwhelmed me with anticipation. I loved every moment being pregnant. I felt well loved by everyone around me. It felt so good, I never worried that something would go wrong. Not knowing the sex of your unborn child makes the birth more like Christmas. I love the surprise of it. To see your child slide out into the world is so overwhelming. He seemed so perfect. To see the child you've been feeling for months is so amazing, you could never be prepared for that moment. Every time I look at him I think, where did you come from? The moment I held him in my arms, it felt so right. I've never been so high. The first night after he was born, I stayed awake all night, just looking at him. The greatest part about nursing is all that time just to look at his little face. I've never seen such perfection. I felt like I knew him the moment we met. I think there's a reason why babies are so dependent on their mothers for such a long time. You need them to need you to learn how to love. Children teach you the responsibility of love. They literally take over your mind when they are little. I love to be needed. It gives life meaning.

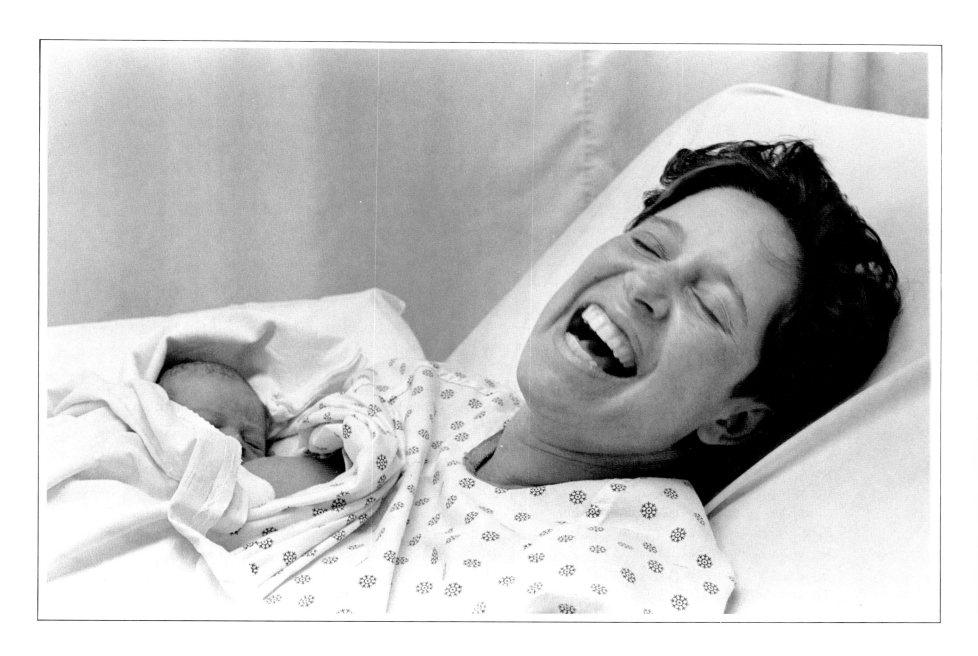

One of the reasons I took the job at the law firm where I now work is I'm hoping it will give me the kind of flexibility I need to raise a family. I'm supposed to take six weeks off, but I don't think it's going to happen. I'm already on the phone a lot. I think I'll be sent work before she's three weeks old. But that's really fine, because I hate to get too out of touch. I've got too much responsibility at work to shut it off for a month. For two years, I worked for a high-pressure law firm where I never got home before eight-thirty at night and I hated myself. One of the reasons I took this job was so I could have some sort of life outside of work.

It was only as I neared thirty that I started to seriously think about being a mother. It was one of the main reasons we got married. In law school I couldn't imagine balancing a legal career with motherhood or wanting to give up the one for the other. Of course, I'm still not sure how I'm going to do some of the juggling I have to do. She's only ten days old. I'll spend my weekends and evenings with her. I hope to bottle feed her in the day and nurse her at night. I didn't take any maternity leave before she was born. I was surprised I panicked as little as I did when I got home from the hospital with her. Other than when she cries for some other reason than hunger, it's a delight to have her around. In some ways it feels like she's always been here.

When my maternity leave is up, I'll definitely go back to work, even if I'm a bit reluctant. I like my work too much to give it up, and I'm not the kind of person who could be happy staying at home. Granted, this is a new thing, but what makes this six weeks especially nice is, it is a finite period of time. I may be wrong, but if I were to stay indefinitely, I think a vague sense of restlessness would spoil the fun. There will be many problems, such as the baby-sitter getting sick, or the baby herself having to go to the doctor, but I feel I can take each challenge as I come to it. My greatest fear right now is having to stay up all night and then have an important meeting in the morning. I know I'll do it. I can't cancel work because I'm sleepy. There's no precedent for a woman of my seniority to have a baby. I get flowers from the office with cards that say, "Hurry back." I do feel a tremendous amount of responsibility to my job as well as to my child. Even in labor, I was worrying about how to reschedule my work the next day. It's all so new. I'm doing these nurturing things, but my identity hasn't changed in two weeks. I still don't think of myself as someone's mother; yet I'm finding myself more interested in things I would never have given a thought to before the baby was born.

My own mother was swayed by the pressure of the fifties. She never worked outside the home after I was born. I sometimes feel a twinge of regret from her that she didn't have the support systems from society back then to keep working while her children were young.

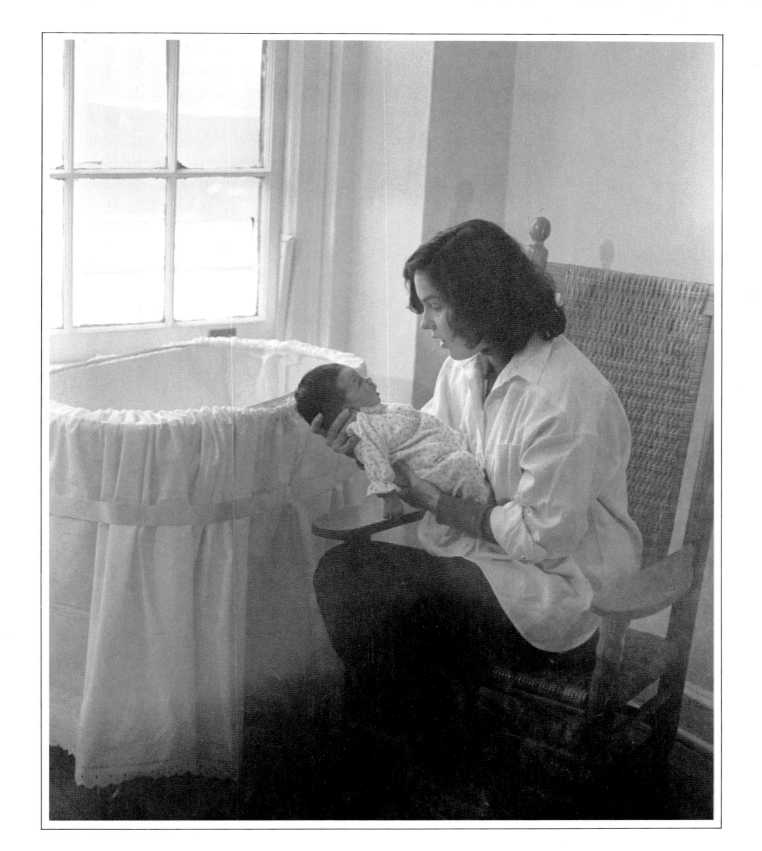

BATHING THE NEWBORN

I love with a fearful love to remember the
first baths I gave this boy—
my second child, so my hands knew what to do,
I laid the tiny torso along my
left forearm, nape of the noodle
neck in the crook of my elbow, hips
tiny as a bird's hips against my wrist, and the
thigh the thickness of a thick pencil held
loosely in the loop of my thumb and forefinger, the
sign that means perfect. I'd soap him slowly, the
long thin cold feet, the
scrotum tight and wrinkled as a rosy
shell so new it was flexible yet, the
miniature underweight athlete's chest, the
gummy furze of the scalp. If I got him too
soapy he'd get so slippery he'd
slide in my grip like an armful of white
buttered noodles, but I'd hold him not too tight,
I knew I was so good for him, and I'd
talk to him the whole time, I'd
tell him about his wonderful body
and the wonderful soap, the whole world made of
    love,
and he'd look up at me, one week old,
his eyes still wide and apprehensive of his
new life. I love that time
when you croon and croon to them, you can see the
calm slowly entering them, you can
feel it in your anchoring hand, the
small necklace of the spine against the
muscle of your forearm, you feel the fear
leaving their bodies, he lay in the blue
oval plastic baby tub and
looked at me in wonder and began to
move his silky limbs at will in the water.

—SHARON OLDS

8

I was sixteen years old when my parents arranged my first marriage. I was not allowed to fall in love. I never was allowed to date or have boyfriends. It's part of the Muslim tradition. I wanted to please my parents, so I married the boy they had chosen for me. I was never in love with him. I don't know how I felt. I was just a child myself. He beat me as soon as we were married. I wasn't allowed to wear makeup or leave the house. Finally, I couldn't take it anymore after being a prisoner for five months. I was three months pregnant when I came back to live at my parents' house. They tried to make me go back to my husband, but I was too scared. It was the most hard part of my life. My husband never came to see me and my mother was very cold toward me. I don't know if she was angry at me for getting pregnant or if she felt sorry for me. Maybe she thought it was her fault. That was a time that I needed her most, but she kept away from me. My sisters told me I'd have to be a prostitute because I could never get married again, because I had a baby. I felt like my life was over—that I could never be happy again. In the seventh month, I remember my milk leaking down from my breast. I told my mother, but she was harsh and angry. I had to keep to myself. I felt ashamed at a time when I should have been proud. I wasn't even allowed to go to my cousin's wedding. It was a shame for my whole family for me to be pregnant and divorced. People accused me of getting married just so I could have a child. I was just obeying my parents. I didn't even know anything about birth control. I was getting really scared by my ninth month. I was terrified to go into labor. I knew I could love the child because it was coming out of me. But I was so worried about how others felt about me. I was in labor for a long, long time. The pain coming and going. My mind was filled with worry and fear. In the hospital they kept me in a darkened room, with all my clothes off. All I could do was grab my belly and scream. The last thing I remember was screaming, screaming—then sleep. When I woke up, they told me I had a baby. I never saw him until the next day. When I saw him, he was beautiful.

The first week home was the most wonderful time of my life. Just being with him, I felt all right again. Looking at him gave me great joy. Even though I know he couldn't understand me, I could talk to him about all my pain and suffering. It made me feel better. He would take his little hand and rest it on my nose and mouth. Then sigh and rest his little head on my shoulder. I felt like he knew everything about me. I felt closer to him than anyone else.

After ten days he became sick. I took him back

to the hospital. They put him through a lot of tests, from the grain of his hair to his toes. He had to stay there, but I was allowed to come in and nurse him. Foam was falling from his mouth, but I never knew he was going to die. When I held him, he would hold his head up, look into my eyes, and cry. When I moved away from him, his head would flop and he'd be silent. He was telling me he was going to leave me. I couldn't believe it, even when my parents brought his little body to my room and put him on my bed. When I touched him and felt the coldness of him, then I finally knew he was gone. I was so sad that he had to leave. I blame myself because during my pregnancy I prayed to the Lord to take my baby away from me if he had to be sick.

I really want to have another child one day, but I'm scared. If I have another boy, I'll name him after my son to give my first child a second chance. I never knew about married love, but I've known a mother's love for her child after only three weeks of being a mother. It's something that was so sweet inside of me that my heart was just marshmallows. For that three weeks I was happy in a way that I'd never known before or since. I want to have a second chance to be a real mother, yet I'm so afraid of being hurt again. I want to feel that sweet loving feeling again.

After about a year of trying to get pregnant, we went to the doctor to see what was wrong. Because my tubes were blocked, I went to a specialist. I had surgery and opened them up. I had an ectopic pregnancy in both tubes in the next six months and had to have them both removed. During the next year I realized my only chance for making a baby now would be in vitro fertilization. I never doubted for a moment that I was going to get pregnant. I enrolled in the clinic in Norfolk. You have to be really determined to have a child to go through the procedures there. Mentally it was the hardest thing I've ever done in my life. You have to wait in line, like cattle, with fifty other girls while they draw your blood every morning. Then you have to drink a lot of water so your bladder will be distended when you have an ultrasound. I'd drive back and forth from my job every day for hormone shots in my hip. Having a baby becomes an obsession. You have to really want that child to go through weeks and weeks of such a demanding medical routine. Emotionally it's draining to know that every woman in the room with you is striving so hard to have what they probably cannot have. All that wanting is almost tangible in the room. Some of those ladies were back after seven or eight previous failures in the program. I was one of the lucky ones who conceived the first month in the program. It's amazing, really, how strong the urge to have a baby can be. I wanted a child so badly. I never could let myself be discouraged. After my fertilized egg was implanted in my uterus, I lay in bed for three days, careful not to nudge it out of place.

After almost three years of trying to conceive, I feel especially fortunate to have a child in my life. It's wonderful that she looks just like my husband. I've never cried like I did when I first held her in my arms. You can't believe that a new life has erupted out of your body.

We decided a long time ago to just have one child. I was a few years older than I planned when I had him because it took a few years to get pregnant, and I had certain career goals I wanted to accomplish before I had a baby. Being an artist is such an insecure profession. I felt I needed to be somewhat established before I became a mother. I needed to know I could count on myself. I had to get over the fear that any distraction would permanently stop me from painting. After I went through lots of ups and downs, I realized that there was something unsatisfying about my career and fifteen years of marriage. My life needed more. I was secure enough in my own identity as an artist to take on a new responsibility.

I seem to be raising my son mostly on instinct. I was afraid I wouldn't know what to do. I'm the kind of person who worries a lot about things ahead of time, and usually they seem a lot easier when they actually happen. My husband gives the bottle, and I nurse him. We take turns changing him and we bathe him together. I still have long periods of time to paint because he's napping a lot in the day. I've always worked in spurts in an intuitively haphazard way, so my concentration hasn't been too disturbed and my life-style hasn't changed very much as a result. After two or three weeks, I went back to teaching again. Even though I don't want to leave the baby, it is very good for me to get the stimulation of the outside world. Even so, I haven't totally escaped postpartum depression. I find myself feeling frustrated that I've lost some part of my freedom— a little bit trapped by breast-feeding, while at the same time I love nursing. Even though my husband and I try to share equal responsibility, if the baby cries in the night, I always hear him first. I think I have a different instinct than my husband, even though he is much more domestic than most men. But I see he is just not as connected to the baby as I am. Carrying a baby inside you for nine months does carry over after it's born.

I had much more simplistic ideas about pregnancy and being a mother until I experienced it myself. I saw my own mother repress everything in her own identity but her role of mother. She is a very talented, artistic person, but it was never encouraged to come out. Her three children are all artists. She is still first and foremost a mother who'd drop anything if her kids needed her, which they still do from time to time. Self-sacrifice is something I find very hard to accept. I really like being a mother, but I never wanted to have a child until I felt really confident that my husband could be around to help me raise him.

I always loved babies, but I was surprised and scared at sixteen to find out I was pregnant. I kept it secret from my own mom as long as I could. I knew I couldn't have an abortion or give it away. Two of my friends had abortions and it just didn't seem right to me. It seemed mean. I can't even give up my stuffed animals. I still sleep with some of them today, so there's no way I could even consider givin' up my baby. It's not easy, though, to be in tenth grade when you're having a baby. I was so sick and tired. Everyone tells me I was a bitch during that time. School didn't work for me anymore after I had a child.

The first year, he cried so much that my mom had to help me a lot. The only time being a mother was like I thought it would be was when he was asleep. My brother and sister always were complaining about his crying. Sometimes it'd seem like he'd never stop. As he got older, he started breaking up everything in the house and that didn't make the rest of the family too happy either. I was trying to go to school and work part-time, as well as do the housework. That was a real bad year for me. All that on top of being stuck with all those needles in the hospital and those labor pains. Ugh! I'll never forget when they cut my bottom open with scissors. Seems like the doctors hurt me much more than the baby. I hobbled around with those stitches for weeks. These are things I wasn't aware of when I used to babysit, before I had a baby of my own.

Seems like it's hard for me to have friends. There's always so much to do around the house. I never like to go out much. I'm too tired at the end of the day. I have my own apartment now and a nice boyfriend. One day I'd like to get married and get a house. There's definitely less pressure on me now that I'm out of my own mother's house. I can't stand to see no one else spank my child. My boyfriend has never left a mark on him, but I have. Even though a child can make you so frustrated, I have no regrets about having him because he loves me so much. That's a real nice feeling. It's hard to get the sassiness out of a kid. It's hard for me to be strict. It makes me feel mean. My own mother used to say, "Give 'em an inch and they'll take a mile." Now I know what she means. My own brothers have been in and out of jail. When I had a boy child, I was so scared. My mom used to always say he'd be just like them and I'd believe her. I felt so hopeless. My boyfriend has lifted me up and given me hope for the future. My child has his own life. He has a chance to make it.

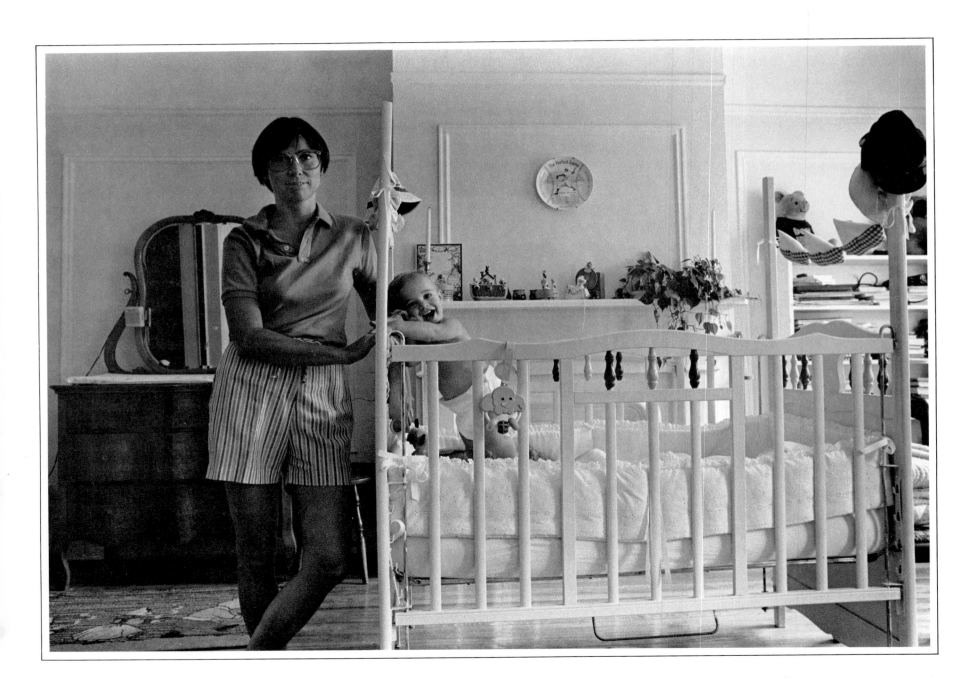

I was the youngest of five. It's funny, but I don't have any clear memory of my own mother when I was little. I guess she was such a constant that I just took her for granted. I used to want a large family too but now that I'm almost thirty-three I feel like two or three kids seems more realistic. Having a child is so much harder than I ever imagined. Who could really describe it? Not only the bad days but the good ones as well. When they are tiny, your relationship with your child is very primal—almost animal-like. I liked it, though the fatigue is a nagging reality. Sometimes when the baby starts his day at five-thirty in the morning, it's hard not to get angry, or at least frustrated. I feel I should let my husband sleep because he goes to work all day. I'm supposed to nap when the baby does, but it rarely works out that way. Even though I have an M.B.A., I never wanted to be chairman of the board, but I wanted to have work outside the house that was meaningful to me. I probably won't go back to work until I've had all my children, so that means I'm on a six- or seven-year leave of absence from the work force. Sometimes I do get lonely for adult conversation during the day, though I do get out of the house a lot and I'm surprised how little I miss my work at the bank. I know I'm in the minority, staying home instead of going back to work. Yet it would seem crazy for me to pay someone else to raise him while I went to work. I wouldn't know what to say to my child when he asked me why I didn't stay home with him. It would seem an incredible statement to a child about his relative importance in my life. At the same time, I think it's not good to be with your child twenty-four hours a day, seven days a week. I'm working on arranging some sort of compromise. We both could use a break from each other. It's so all encompassing now, it's easy to forget that our children are so dependent for just a short time. They do eventually grow up.

19

While I was pregnant I dreamed I gave birth to a little girl who looked just like my husband. She even had his glasses. I think I was fearful of inherited characteristics that I couldn't control. When she was born, her face looked so familiar to me I felt like I already knew her.

The first year of her life, I felt like all my energy was going exclusively into her. Even though it was exhausting, I really liked the feeling of being so involved. Sometimes my frustration from being overwhelmed would be directed toward my husband more than the baby. It forced us to talk about our feelings a lot and now I feel we're closer than ever. My attachment to my daughter made me worry that perhaps I'd emotionally set my husband aside. It takes a while to get your marriage back in balance after you have a baby.

I think I feel more confident about myself now. I'm tapping inner resources that haven't been called upon before. I don't feel threatened about losing my professional identity if I stop work to have a child, because I feel it's the most rewarding and important way for me to spend my time. When people ask, "What do you do?", what they want to know is how much money you make, not how you really spend your time. I'm fortunate enough to be able to work at home, so I don't have to make the difficult choice of being economically dependent or leaving my baby in someone else's care all day.

The most immediate reward of mothering is the physical relationship. It's wonderful to be touched all day. The nighttime feedings were a wonderful time of physical closeness. It's a pleasure. Nursing is more than a balanced diet. It's also a warm, loving bond. All those hours of physical intimacy in the first year or two are bound to have a positive influence on your future relationship with your child.

I needed a family. I was alone in a Spanish-speaking neighborhood, estranged from my own family. I worked with institutionalized children and it was hard—I couldn't help them as much as I'd like to. This was a wanted child. When I was pregnant, my grandmother was dying and the baby growing inside me was something to take me forward. I felt better about myself than I had in a long time. More balanced. We'd like to leave the city and go to the islands. Both of us have a rural background. Now we're living one day at a time. We are anarchists, but have a commitment to this child. Mothering is really a positive way to channel my creative energy.

I can see people get offended when they see me with my baby. You can see the racism run through them, both black and white. It's a terrible ignorance. I know I've got to be really strong to combat the irrational hatred. I have a vision for a better day on this planet. It takes faith. I was at the point of being very disillusioned and bitter until I got pregnant. Then I was forced to change—there was potential again.

I always listen to my intuition. Sometimes it's hard when people say, "How could you?" but I just return to my heart and listen.

When I first found out I was pregnant, it was a disaster. The father of the child and I had parted and gone our separate ways before I knew I was pregnant. Everyone was encouraging me to have an abortion. I didn't want to do that. Having an abortion felt unjustifiable, because I respected the life of the child much more than my own fears about what to do. Just as God granted life to this child, I felt it was against God's will to have an abortion. After a couple of months of confusion, I realized that I could take my mistake and transform it into a wonderful gift for a couple who were unable to conceive. I consciously decided to perceive my situation as a blessing, instead of a tragedy. I shed tears many, many times in the process of deciding what was best for both my child and me.

I felt I had a deep responsibility for this child to have a peaceful, loving birth. The child's birthing was the most beautiful day of my life. I love that child infinitely, though we are physically not together now. "Love is reaching out, opening up and letting go. Love is giving up the only thing we truly own." To me, the only thing we truly own is ourselves, and in bringing the child lovingly into the world, my total desire was to be selfless. Making the decision about where the child was to be (with me or with an adopting couple) was very difficult, so I left my spirit open for God to guide me to the answer. The answer did unfold itself, for the child to go to an adopting couple who were longing for a child. I am this child's birth mother, but another woman will raise him, and be his mother.

For three years now, not a day has gone by that I haven't confronted a sense of loss, as well as a sense of appreciation of knowing he is with a good, loving family. I don't regret giving him up for adoption, yet I'm sorry I didn't make some sort of agreement with the adoptive parents to keep in touch once a year. It's hard not knowing how he's doing, as any mother would feel. I just want to know that he's okay and healthy. My baby will always be in my prayers, even when I am able to raise other children of my own. I want adopted children everywhere to know that they were not rejected by their birth mothers and that we deeply love and care about their well-being . . . forever.

My own mother didn't work, but she was in a social position of having to do a lot of entertaining. She ran a staff of five servants in a thirty-five room house. She entertained at least four nights a week. Her role was much more that of her husband's social partner than my mother. My earliest visual memory of her was in a long black dressing gown in the living room playing the piano. Being her only child, we've always been close, and we're even more so now that I have a child myself. What's really strange to me is even though I had a nanny until I was five, I don't remember her at all.

It's always been really important to me to make money so that I can remain financially independent and maintain a life-style to which I am accustomed. I'm never going to inherit any money, so if I want it, I've got to make it. I love my work. Having my own business gives me tremendous satisfaction. It's my other child. Work satisfies another part of me from the challenges of motherhood. When I go on vacation, I miss my work but I don't miss my child at work. Very early on after my son was born, I taught myself how to compartmentalize my life. At home I don't think about work, and at work I don't think about home. It's the only way I can stay sane and do a good job in both the marketplace and my domestic life. I wouldn't have had a child if I felt that I'd have to give up my career. I feel children are very versatile and can readily adapt to many different kinds of living environments. In the morning,

he's used to me going to work. He practically shoves me out the door. He has his own routines and his day. No matter how many hours a day you spend with your child, it seems mothers are always worried that they're not doing enough for their children. There's nothing wrong with feeling guilty; it's probably a prime motivation in getting things done. The job of raising children is so difficult and there's no test or report card along the way. Children are so individual. What is good for one doesn't pertain to the other. They train the mother how to behave.

Being an only child, I was totally intimidated by this tiny creature. What inspires anyone to have a child? I think it takes two years to comprehend the responsibility and grow to understand your baby. The physical and emotional drain is something you can't be prepared for. The first year after my son was born, I felt like I lived my life in fifteen-minute increments. Fifteen minutes to do this, then fifteen minutes to do that. Time is stretching out now. I have an hour here, then an hour there. But there's never enough time. The hardest adjustment for me was getting used to having no personal time. No time to write letters or take a long bath. Even walking down the street loses its pleasure when you know the babysitter is wondering where you are. Although I miss my personal freedom, I have no regrets.

I think our society has a peculiar attitude toward mothering. Everyone believes the first two

years of life are the most important time in our development. Who wrote that on stone? There is too much emphasis put on the problems of child rearing. Every normal feeling becomes a syndrome. Mothers in one sense or another have always worked. The upper class always had nurses to raise their children and the working-class women were caretakers for those children. Women have always worked, but what's new is that women are attaining traditionally male roles of status and power in the marketplace.

When I was a young girl, I wanted ten children. That was before I realized the difficulty in running a household full of small children. Also, I still have to work to help support the family financially. It seems to me, at least when they're young, the housework and the financial burden are the most frustrating parts of mothering. It's so difficult when it's time to go to work, the house is a mess, and all three children need something from me at once. I spend about twenty hours a week as a nurse in a hospital. I enjoy it when I'm there, but I don't think I'd be working outside the house if we didn't really need the money. I do like my job because I always feel I've made a difference to somebody just by being there. Being a mother isn't always as immediately rewarding. Young children aren't as appreciative of the care I give them as my elderly patients. I think nursing has had a positive effect on my mothering. It teaches you to put the needs of others before your own. One thing you never hear or read about in books is the loss of sleep you suffer when you have little children. I'm sure I haven't had one night's sleep uninterrupted by at least one of them in seven years. It seems their needs are almost more than I can give. Yet I'd feel guilty to ask my husband to help at night because he works so many hours at the hospital as a doctor. He's already on call a lot. When the children cry out in the night, I'm the one who hears them. I wouldn't work nights for that reason; he'd sleep right through their cries. Sometimes it's frustrating because I feel his job as a pediatrician is generally considered more important than my job as mother and nurse.

I wasn't prepared for how physically demanding raising children is. I had no idea I'd ever be so overwhelmed that I couldn't even read a book. When they are all asleep at the same time, there's so much housework to be done, but I'm too tired to do anything but sleep myself. Strangely enough, though, this is probably the happiest time in my life. I was the youngest child and I used to pray every night for God to send my mother a baby. I felt I had all this nurturing to give and no place to put it. The love you give your children is like black paper; it absorbs and you can't immediately see it, but you know it's there. Your friends and husband are more like a mirror. The love you give them reflects back more immediately.

I worked for the phone company for fourteen years before I had children. When I started I was an operator, and then became a telephone linesman and installer. Eventually I was a supervisor with an all-male crew. I was the token female. At the time, I never realized what a pioneer I was. I was just interested in making more money. I got paid much less teaching installation than when I became an installer myself. It never occurred to me that I couldn't do anything a man could do. I'm five-nine and weighed one hundred forty pounds. So I could hold my own. I always enjoyed my work. It was more than just a way to make a dollar. I was good at it and I enjoyed it, but it was never my primary identity. When I wasn't working, I was free of the job. It's one hundred percent easier to be out in the work world than to stay at home raising small children. I always felt I could do any job I put my mind to. It's not so easy to be a mother. All the practice in the world doesn't always make you good at it. It's much more introspective work. You constantly question your judgment. I felt a lot more confident about my skills at the phone company. Since I've had children, I'm much harder on myself. I'm more aware of myself and feel I know myself better now. I've never been much of a housewife, even now that I quit working.

It was hard for me to learn to be financially dependent on my husband. I always felt good about being able to take care of myself. I didn't like the idea of having to ask my husband for money. I had hired a sitter to come in and care for my first child when she was three months old, so I could go back to work. I felt this tremendous sense of loss. I wasn't prepared for being so torn. So I decided to stay home with her and I found myself a full-time house-wife for the first time. After my second child was born, I began to really miss that sense of satisfaction that comes from being outwardly productive, even though I found mothering very emotionally satisfying. I feel like I'm a guide for my children. I don't tell them how to behave as much as try to live an example. Having children makes me very aware of the necessity of exchange in life: to never take without giving something back. It was sometimes hard for me to be unemployed because it's hard to see on a daily basis what you are contributing in your life. There's no finished product to see and you don't get much admiration from others. The rewards of staying at home are certainly no less important, but they are less tangible. I wasn't prepared for my change of status at first, but now I'm at the point where I'm learning how to work out of the house part-time and still spend a majority of my time with my two children. It's a constant juggling act to meet my kids' needs and still find a personal sense of satisfaction in work outside of my family life.

Being a mother is the best thing that has ever happened to me. It's taught me never to underestimate a human being. I've also learned to respect the

skill of communication. It's the key to all relation-
ships. I always look forward to the future. It excites
me to think about what I can do better, look forward
to, and create. That's the whole thing of life. Life is
overcoming barriers and doing new things. It's as
simple as that. If I ever look back, it's only to realize
how fast the time's gone.

I don't think loving your child is always instinctual. My second child was unplanned and I was resentful toward her when she was born. I held her because I felt I should, not because I wanted to. Yet within a week I found myself intrigued with this new little person. Soon I was madly in love, kissing her every chance I could. My relationship with my own two daughters has had a big impact on my feelings toward my own mother. I was rebellious as a child. I can remember avoiding her touch. When I think of my daughter treating me like that, it makes me feel so appreciative of my mother's loving. She was so supportive and involved with me and I was always fighting like hell to separate from her while I was growing up. Now that I'm a mother myself, I'm as conservative as my own mother was.

Having children has changed my relationship with God as well. Spiritually, I'm incredibly awed by His love. My children are His gift. They are not mine to own, I merely care for them. They are God's children and they live by the grace of God.

This is the way I understand things in life that otherwise seem so unfair. All things in life are a direct result of His will. For every action there's an equal and opposite reaction. There could be no joy without suffering and that balance of opposites is the harmony of God's will. That doesn't mean I'm completely free of responsibility for my children's happiness. I still have freedom of choice to make the right or wrong decision in raising them. I could inadvertently go against God's will. Knowing God's will is a personal experience. Consider "luck" just another word for "grace."

When you have the responsibility of raising children, you realize that your thoughts and ideas are not enough. You have to follow your beliefs with action. Children learn by observing what you do, not just listening to what you say. Realizing this has helped me try a little harder in my own life. I feel more aware, more connected to myself since I've become a mother.

I'm twenty-six years old. I had my first child at twenty-two and my baby last year. I always wanted to be a doctor when I was a little girl and I'm far from it! I liked the idea of caring for people and getting prestige for the work. What I really need is being with people, so as office manager of a health club I'm fulfilling that need. I meet a wide variety of people every day. I stopped working when my oldest child was born. After the second baby came, I began to feel I was suffering from brain rot. Being around small children all day was making me feel isolated and frustrated. My husband works at night so he can be with the children. His mother helps too. I owe a lot to them both for helping me get out of the house and back in the world. I think a family structure to fall back on is missing for so many mothers of young children.

Both my husband and I have strong family ties. We live with his parents and his mother is a great help to me. My own mother lives nearby and there's no one in this world who means more to me. We talk every day. She's the one who taught me that nothing is out of reach. I try to give my own children the same gift. I don't want to protect my children as much as teach them, prepare them for the facts of life. I don't think children should be put in a protective shell. Even as a child, I longed to be an adult. I hated being condescended to, with no say-so over my own destiny. Having a child of my own was the best thing that ever happened to me. I loved the responsibility. After my second child was born, it seemed like child care became never ending and there was no time for myself. Getting a job out of the house for the afternoon has helped me get back in touch with myself. Now that my husband helps out, since I too work out of the house, I think he has more respect for the work women do. As I get older, I am getting more and more ambitious. I want to go back to school and have a career in social work after my girls are in school. Unlike so many of my friends, I don't have any desire for them to stay babies.

My own mother died when I was pregnant. I quit working and read every book about pregnancy and birth that I could get my hands on. It was like preparing for the toughest role of my life. I'd been acting professionally for about twelve years and I felt like my career was at a secure enough place so I could have a child. I was very close to my own mother and my pregnancy helped pull me through her death.

Sometimes my daughter reminds me of my own mother to the point that I look at her and say, "Mother, are you there?" I was working on a film and I was tired and depressed. My little girl toddled over with the Bible and said, "Here, Mom, read this. It'll make you feel better. It's about God." She was only two and had never even been to Sunday school. It was really strange. I felt the loving presence of my own mother really strong then. Most of the time she reminds me of myself when I was little. It makes me feel great.

I got so involved in her after she was born I had a hard time giving interviews because all I wanted to talk about was giving birth or nursing her. I got an offer for the lead role in *Terms of Endearment* when she was seven months old, but I couldn't bear to leave her. I have no regrets, though. I felt like I was in the right place at the right time with her. When my baby was a little over a year, I chose to play the mother in the film *The River*. I felt like she was a character who could also take real good care of my little girl. I was still nursing her and brought her to the set with me every day. I felt like I had a new level of understanding in playing the role of mother. I'd played that role before but always related it to my own childhood. It was different this time.

Being a mother really keeps you honest. I strive to be as good a mother as my own. She was so patient and loving. When I went to New York to seek my fortune, she would say, "It's just a matter of time, honey." All my life she told me I was special, and I guess I believed her.

When my second son was born, it wasn't apparent that he had problems until he was about a month old. As the weeks went by, he became less and less active. Testing revealed a rare genetic syndrome that involves the kidneys, eyes, and brain. It's an X-linked trait carried on the mother's side. I felt so bad about myself because it was my gene that caused these problems. I felt I wasn't allowed, as the mother, to have any negative feelings about my child. I felt so guilty about my disappointment, but therapy gave me permission to accept my feelings and deal with them. At first it was really hard on my self-image to have a handicapped child. I tended to obsess on my baby's imperfections and lose sight of the fact that I also had an intelligent, physically perfect son as well. It took over a year for me to get through a phase of self-recrimination and go on to living a more balanced family life.

Even though I no longer blame myself for his handicaps, our life is still a series of acceptances and losses. A particularly painful period for me was when he reached eighteen months and my neighbors' children started doing all the adorable things that toddlers do and he remained infantile. It's been a real lesson in patience for me to have to wait two years to get much response from my baby. Now he cuddles and smiles back at me. Believe me, the hugs and smiles are especially appreciated when they are such a long time coming. It's still hard for my husband to be close to this baby because, like many men, he doesn't truly warm up to his children until they are past infancy. My older healthy son is much more emotionally accessible to him.

One pleasant surprise for me is how this baby, as sick as he has been, has really filled a place for his older brother. They have a very affectionate relationship. We're becoming a close-knit family again for the first time since the baby was born. When either one of them is out of the house, I miss them both the same, but for different reasons. The physical contact you have with a handicapped child is tremendous because they remain a baby for such a long time. My older child is a great strength to me emotionally. I can really appreciate his mental and physical abilities. I have a different perspective about life now. I have a deeper appreciation of things I used to take for granted and a stronger ability to accept the things I cannot change. I've had to face so many painful truths in the last few years, I'm probably a lot more honest. One of my biggest fears is that my baby will outlive his family. As long as I'm around, I know he'll be taken care of. His death would hurt me a lot, but it wouldn't be the same loss as the death of a healthy child.

The pain of having a chronically ill child never goes away. You learn to accept it, but it keeps on hurting in the same spot. It's a tremendous price to pay for whatever wisdom you gain. I'd trade that wisdom any day for a chance for my son to get well.

My decision to get married was strongly influenced by my desire to have children. In seventh grade I was asked to draw a picture of what I wanted to be when I grew up. My drawing showed me with seven children. I even had them all named! Now that I'm expecting my third child, I'll see how that feels before I have any more. There's nothing I've ever found that is more deeply satisfying than nurturing small children, but it is often difficult to maintain my own sense of self-esteem. Child care involves a lot of servitude. It seems like you're always serving others. It's always, "Mommy I want this, Mommy I need that!" Sometimes it's hard to maintain that sense of self beyond "Mommy," to stay in touch with the person I was before I had children. The hardest thing about being a mother is the lack of recognition for the worth of the job. The respect you do get seems condescending. When people ask me if I work, I say, yes, I take care of my children. It's very difficult in today's economy to live on one income, but we feel that the work I do at home is more important than any job I could have in the outside world. In a way, I feel the low status of motherhood is a backlash of the women's movement. I left no great career opportunities behind. To pay another woman to do the work I now do and enjoy at home makes no sense. It's taken me years of nurturing to get to know myself, my strengths and weaknesses. I can imagine being a midwife sometime in the future when my children no longer need full-time supervision. I was not ready to take such responsibility before I had children but I know I now am.

When I was growing up, the women in my family had total responsibility for running the household. I think there was more equality in the past when men and women worked together side by side in order to feed themselves. They were really sharing their lives. Progress has actually separated the sexes. Equality is a media lie. When women leave the house all day and leave their children in the hands of someone else all day, the quality of the family life suffers. I know I'm out of sync with the times feeling this way, but superwoman is a myth. Children need more than a few hours of "quality time." If the mother is gone most of the day, I can't help but feel that the child feels the loss. When I was twenty-five I worked in an office and had my own secretary. So what? This job seems much more worthwhile to me. It's a shame that mothers don't get respect in a man's world. My own mother always seemed so helpless to me, so I decided early on to take care of myself. Even as a child, I supported myself. This is the first time since I was very little that I've been dependent on anyone, but in the back of my mind I know I could go out and get a job if I had to. Remember, mothers who work always have to hire another woman to come into their home to do the work they left behind. I wonder why it is that all the advice books deal with the problems of mothering. No one ever talks about the joy. The feeling that it gives you is almost like a secret. It's so intense, so special it almost defies conversation. The emotions are passionate. Being a mother of small children puts you in a club of mutual understanding. If you have to go back to work six weeks after the baby is born, you probably don't allow yourself to feel those things.

After you've stayed home with a small child for a couple of years, you can't help but have a profound respect for what women do. There is nothing more exhausting than a twenty-four-hour, seven-day-a-week responsibility for another human being. Being there for them has got to make a difference. Children are small for a short, short part of your life. The time goes by before you know it.

When I got married, I had a job but no career. I was raised to get married and be a wife and mother. I always felt that was my station in life. I want to teach my three girls that marriage and motherhood is not the beginning and not the end of life. I want them to have more options than I felt I did. A housewife is a career that should be chosen as one of many options. I have terrible regrets that my parents didn't raise me that way. I have terrible regrets that I didn't consider other options for my life. It gives me problems in my relationship with my children. Sometimes I feel trapped or resentful. I'm stuck between a rock and a hard place because I deeply love my children, yet I'm not sure if being a housewife and mother is what I'm best suited to do.

When you have a baby, it takes quite a few years to realize what a lifelong responsibility they are. The job is so big, it's difficult to comprehend. If you get burned out, too bad. You can't get fired or quit. Then you feel like something's really wrong with you if you feel that way. I don't really enjoy what I'm doing now. I'm tired of domestic duties, but I'm not sure how to fix it yet. I lack the mental discipline to achieve and compete in a man's world. Like so many women, I never even played team sports. Even though I graduated from college, I never was trained in any skills to have a career in the outside world. I truly believed that I'd fall in love, get married, have children, and live happily ever after. I wish I could be more accepting. I question everything. I have difficulty postponing gratification. No one ever told me that life was a struggle, so my own life has caught me by surprise. Sometimes I cannot cope. Everything that's supposed to make me happy is hard. Raising a family is the hardest job in the world.

All my life I was so focused on being a daughter, a wife, and a mother that I've never really known who in the world I was. I've always done what I felt was expected of me. I have a lot of guilt over not being good enough at any of my three roles. I want everything to be perfect, but it's not. Right now I've got a lot of anger. I feel very, very frustrated.

I have a really hard time getting along with my

oldest daughter. Sometimes I feel a little jealous of her. She's very smart and beautiful and society will offer her a lot more opportunities than I had. At the same time, I try to live my life through her. Of course, it makes it hard on both of us when she screws up. Half of me wants her to be everything I couldn't be, and the other half is resentful that she has the chance.

After my third child was born, I felt so closed in that I slipped a note under my husband's office door and walked out of the house. I came back that night because I knew there was no other place where I belonged. I didn't want to fail. Five years later, I'm still trying to make things work. Admitting that you have to turn your back on your family doesn't get you a lot of sympathy. Fathers walk out the door all the time and it's not nearly as scandalous as when a mother does. We're supposed to be naturally self-sacrificing.

After my first son was born, I had two miscarriages. When I got pregnant with my triplets, it was a planned pregnancy, though I didn't plan on three babies. When the doctor told me I was carrying three, I felt the blood leave my face and my life started passing before my eyes. My mind filled with a thousand questions and then I got excited. I was immediately confined to bed and had to quit work. This was November and I wasn't due until June. I didn't want to miscarry for a third time, so I did as I was told. I was so afraid I was going to lose them. After a few months, my belly was so large I couldn't get around if I wanted to. My three-year-old wasn't in school yet, so it was hard taking care of him when I was supposed to stay in bed. It was hard on my marriage too. We couldn't make love the whole pregnancy. Now I'm so petrified of getting pregnant I don't know what to do.

All those months that I had to stay inside and grow these babies, my mind never sat still. I sat in my rocker every day until I was put in the hospital because of early contractions. I was given medication every two hours around the clock so it was impossible to get any good sleep. After four weeks of no sleep and getting sick from the medication, I was more than ready to get them out as soon as I could. They were born by cesarean, because one was transverse. The first time I tried to feed them, it took me forty-five minutes with each baby. I felt completely defeated. Each time got better until I felt more under control. I'd nurse two, one at a time, and give the third a bottle every four hours. I had to schedule them right away. Nursing on demand was impossible with three of them. Eventually I could feed all three in forty-five minutes.

Having triplets gives you an instant large family. I remember seeing women with twins and wondering how they coped. I've been too busy to feel victimized. It's forced me to look at the bright side of things. We have our health and we have each other. Not that I don't often feel overwhelmed. Sometimes my apartment looks like an Excedrin commercial. When all four of them are crying at once, I have to remind myself that it'll be quiet again soon. I'm a much more organized person than I ever was before. I feel like nothing is too much for me now. I have much more confidence in myself now than I did four years ago.

When I'm forty-five, they're gonna be twenty-one and seventeen and I'm going to be on a cruise ship to nowhere. My fantasies keep me going through the hard times. That, and the love I have for each of them, can sustain a lot. I love them more than my own life. I thank God every day for what he gave me.

I always tried to do well in anything I did. I've been accused of being a perfectionist. I think it pleased my parents. Being the oldest, I was very much like my father. When I was very young I was a real tomboy, yet as I got older I got more and more confident in being feminine. Now I can see a lot of my own mother in my personality. Yet when I look at my own children, it's hard to see myself in them. My two boys are so demanding and active right now. I can't imagine having another child anytime soon; yet I do sometimes want to have a daughter. There's something so special about being a woman —something you just can't pass on to your boys. If I never have a daughter, that's what I'll miss.

I think the most important thing I can teach my children is a respect for others and themselves. If they know they are loved, they'll be able to love others. Because I'm such a perfectionist, I've spent the last four years giving everything to my children. I've never missed taking time for myself because I always wanted to be with my children, probably because I remember my own mother being available to me when I needed her. I know that as they get older they'll need me less and less, and I'll have more time for myself. It's not always easy. Not a day goes by when I don't doubt my ability to be a good mother. People give me advice to leave my children and don't worry if they scream and cry for me, but my heart won't let me do it. All the advice in the world doesn't make me feel more comfortable. I have to trust my own instincts, even if they are contrary to well-meaning advice. I probably get my insecurity about mothering because I feel it's so important. It's the most important thing I'll ever do. My children are a gift that is an enormous responsibility. My teachings now can help them not succumb to the horrible depravity I see in the world. At the same time, I know my control over them is limited in the long run, that fate does take a part in everyone's life. It's certainly much easier to decide to have a child than it is to decide how to raise them. The difficulties of daily life make it difficult to always remember what an honor it is.

49

Getting pregnant with this baby didn't just happen to me. I was really ready. I was only thirteen when I had my older son and it didn't dawn on me that I was really responsible for him. I was just a child myself. My mother and sister practically raised him the first three years. My mom raised ten herself. I always had to be responsible for my mother's babies. Seemed like every year there was another one coming. I was glad to have my mama help me with my first, but fourteen years later I was really ready to take responsibility for my little girl myself. I have enjoyed her so much. I missed out on a lot of things with my boy. I was growing up myself. I don't know if I remember when he started crawling, but with my daughter I really notice all those things. Watching her grow, learning to walk and talk, she makes me feel things that I've never been able to feel before. I feel so lucky to have her. I'm more aware of things that go on in life. I don't take anything for granted.

My boyfriend wanted this baby as much as I did. He wants more. I won't marry my baby's daddy unless he gets baptized. I've been talking to him a lot about it lately. If he can make that kind of commitment to God, then I could trust him more. I'd like more kids too, but not without a husband. Both of us work real hard, and I'd like to build a home.

It's a lot harder to be poor in money—but I don't feel poor in my feelings and love. I'm not greedy but sometimes I feel guilty that I don't have more money to spend on my kids.

My own mother had all the responsibility for raising us. She was a strong woman. I used to feel I didn't need a man to raise a child, but now I think it's better to have someone I can care for and that cares for me. All the men I knew in the past have just been disappointments. I haven't been putting too much hope in finding someone who would really commit himself to raising a child.

When I was pregnant with my first child, I was really dissatisfied with the condescending attitudes toward giving birth. The male, institutional orientation toward management of labor and delivery seemed negative, even potentially destructive toward good mothering. I think how one gives birth really influences your early relationship with your child, which is the foundation for a lifetime. If you're strapped down in a powerless position and treated by the staff like an incompetent, it doesn't instill much confidence in a young mother. As a result, breast-feeding is not as successful and a cycle of frustration and failure is begun. I regret weaning my oldest child as early as I did, but I had so much pressure from society to do so. I decided to follow my own heart with the next child and she's still nursing at two and a half alongside her baby sister. Although it's demanding to nurse a toddler, I feel she'd be a lot more difficult if she were denied my breast because she can still rely on me for comfort.

It's odd that in our society we spend the first three years of our children's lives trying to make them independent, and the next fifteen years complaining about how independent they are.

Patience is a key virtue for being a good mother. Mothering three children under four is a real lesson in patience. If I want to do anything for myself, I have to wait until late at night. I let my babies sleep with me in bed at night, so I don't have to keep getting up. When they wake, I simply nurse them back to sleep without having to really wake up. The children sleep through light and noise because they're used to it. I believe the primary way that the human mother is supposed to interact with her small child is through nursing. Our culture tolerates breast-feeding as nutrition for the first few months, but we are not ready to acknowledge the emotional benefits. There is a big difference between nursing and breast-feeding.

I got pregnant a couple of hours after I got married. I always assumed I'd have children. That was a major reason for getting married. I wanted my parents to enjoy being grandparents while they were still young. I was surprised how easy it was to conceive. If I don't use birth control, I get pregnant. Sometimes I get pregnant even when I do use it. When my first son was two, I got pregnant with triplets. I was totally shocked. I couldn't believe this was happening to me. Then I wanted to tell everyone. I was more excited than horrified. I didn't know about all the medical complications involved in multiple pregnancies. If I was carrying triplets today, I'd be petrified with worry for their well-being. It was a hard time for me. With so many complications, I had a lot of time to think because of the enforced bed rest. It was hard on my older child. He didn't understand what was wrong with his mom. I felt bad for him. I don't like to think back on that time because I feel like it was sort of a failure. I'll see another mother with healthy twins walking together and it's like grieving. I have a fantasy of three little babies in their high chairs and the reality of two girls having so many problems to overcome. That's hard for me.

It's funny, I didn't openly grieve for the triplet that died because I was so concerned over the survival of the other two. It's like I had to do something, and failed. During the days when I had to stay in bed, both during the bleeding in the first trimester and after the membranes ruptured in the seventh month, all I could think of was: "Hold on, hold on." Every day I marked off the calendar was a success for me, yet deep down I knew that something wasn't right. I would go over the delivery in my mind, what it would be like, how the babies would be, and in my mind all three of them were okay—I was so shocked that one was stillborn. That was a terrible time in my life. The first months were so hard when the two girls had to stay in the hospital. Every morning I'd call the nurses to check on them. It was so difficult to be separated from them. It was all I could do to tear myself away and take care of my little boy. I was always worried that something was wrong with one of the twins. It was about a year when her cerebral palsy was diagnosed. Cerebral palsy is such a catch-all description that I hardly knew how to react. The handicap becomes more obvious as a child tries to do more things. Physical therapy makes a difference, but there are no guarantees and it's hard to know how much progress is possible. It dawned on me very slowly, the extent of her handicaps. No one really knows when she'll be up and walking. I know in my heart that she'll be able to get out of a wheelchair eventually. Soon after the handicap was diagnosed, I got pregnant again. It was a total accident. I feel like maybe my subconscious really wanted me to have a baby to replace the triplet I lost. I think to myself—in six months I'll have my triplets, they'll all be the same size.

I might end up adopting some handicapped children at some point in my life. Now knowing what I know and seeing what I see—to grow up handicapped is hard, but to grow up handicapped without your parents is totally unfair. It happens all the time—children rejected by their families because they're not perfect. So many kids that could be worthwhile people if given half a chance. Granted, handicapped children are more work, yet they can give you so much in return for the time you invest. Everyone has a different reality. A handicapped child should not feel the world owes him something.

I think it's especially good for handicapped children to have siblings because it takes the focus off the handicap.

I was totally unprepared for motherhood. I guess most women are. The biggest surprise for me was what hard, physical work it is. Yet I'm so overwhelmed at the love that grows between you and each child. Your love for your children is different than other attachments. They are a part of you. It's almost like loving yourself. You couldn't love anyone else in such an unconditional way.

55

My oldest child was a toddler and I was just at the point that I thought I could be a "perfect" mother when I unexpectedly became pregnant with twins. I knew my expectations of control over my life would soon be lost. Both elated and terrified, I think I laughed and cried at the same time. As I suspected, having a child under two and infant twins was not easy. I was too exhausted to even think about the situation. The first year or so my personality changed a lot. The fatigue and the unrelenting drudgery of the work made me feel very resigned and passive. My best friends said they hardly knew me. I'll never forget what a strain that first year was, with three tiny children. There was a lot of outside pressure from other mothers to give my oldest child time I simply didn't have because of the physical demands of two tiny infants. I got to the point where I really fantasized leaving my whole life behind—just walking out the door. These feelings are stressful on a marriage as well as on the quality of your mothering. Time healed many of the problems. It was much easier for me once they were able to entertain themselves. Now I really enjoy them. For me, it's a real luxury to stay at home with my children and have time to go on picnics, go swimming, do arts and crafts. I even chose a preschool where I can participate in a lot of the activities, because I really do enjoy them. Since I've had children I've really widened my outlook toward life. Now I probably have a larger circle of friends than I did before I was a mother and my marriage has a deeper level of security since we've weathered the years when they were babies. We both enjoy being a family— it feels good. I have enough confidence in myself now to leave the child-care books on the shelf and be more relaxed about the appropriateness of my responses. I get a lot of satisfaction and support getting together with other women and their small children. We can laugh about the fantasy of perfection and control that we were trying to achieve. I remember thinking my mother looked awful in the morning and I said to myself, "I'll never be like that." Then one morning I got up and looked in the mirror and there she was!

My family has been Mennonite for generations. Our community has its own schools and work to keep from becoming too worldly. A Christian education for our children is important to us. Family and God are the centers of my life. It's not uncommon to see six to ten children in a Mennonite family, even though birth control is not considered a sin.

I could say that my role of mother is a calling. Although I'm not beyond frustration, I'm proud of the job. More than that, I feel like I'm fulfilling God's will. My own mother taught me cooking, sewing, and gardening. I'm from a family of thirteen children myself. I truly believe that God guides our way and keeps His eye over us. We're born and have life to bring honor to God. My ability to serve Him reflects in everything I do, including my relationship with my family. I don't look at death as an end, but rather a passing from this life to another, better life. I consider the struggle of life a privilege. It's our opportunity to glorify Him by living according to His word in the Bible. There have been times when I've wondered what life's all about. My faith is deeper than just wearing plain clothes. It's serving Christ that makes life meaningful. That's why I like being a mother because I serve my children.

I'm much more understanding of my own mother now that I have children of my own. I never really wanted children, yet I suspected I would someday. I struggled against that expectation for a long time. I was even a member of a non-parent group. We felt that motherhood should be optional. Now, I certainly hope that my children have children. I don't know many people who are interested in children who aren't their own. I was married six years before I had my first child.

I used to bridle at the title Mother, yet the more I lived with it, the more comfortable I became with the term. I thought that I would be less attractive, have fewer professional opportunities if that was my major role. I resist the idea that biology is destiny, though now I'm much more comfortable with the differences between men and women. It keeps things interesting. I've always been amazed how individual my children are. I see qualities in them that I know didn't come from me, that I'd be incapable of teaching them. It's almost impossible to separate the nature from the nurture. I have high expectations for myself as a painter and as a mother—guilt motivates me to get as much done as I do. I keep running back and forth, always feeling guilty about what I'm not doing. Right now I feel my painting is suffering. My daughters are very interested in painting. They say they want to be artists and I'm not sure I like that. I want them to have work that they love but I also want them to be able to support themselves financially.

As a little girl, I wanted to be a boy. I played with guns, I dressed like a boy and kept my hair short. I hated dolls. I realize now that I felt this way because it seemed to me that men had more status and power, and that appealed to me. During the last few years of my marriage, my husband was more like a third child than a helpmate. He seemed to be growing younger, depending on me for everything, whereas my babies were growing up and becoming more independent. Watching them grow up and away from me was a revelation to me. I thought, so that's what life is all about—mutual independence instead of dependence. After the divorce I realized there was nothing I couldn't do. It was tricky learning to make final decisions, but I soon learned that I could rely on myself.

I've gone through so many profound changes since my children were babies. It took me ten years of marriage to discover my own needs and opinions. At thirty-two I discovered I had cancer. I had a breast removed but was able to walk away with my life. I never really believed I would die because I didn't feel sick. Instead of feeling sorry for myself, I feel lucky that I still have my health and so do my children. I wish my memory was better. Life is so short. Even though my children are still young, I've already forgotten a lot about their babyhood. My own mother always told me not to have children because it was such a thankless job. As a result, I've been pleasantly surprised by the many pleasures of raising children. Once you realize how little you can ultimately control them, watching them grow and guiding them can be an exciting adventure.

As a little girl, I never was encouraged to do much musically. My parents told me I couldn't carry a tune. My husband was the musician in the family. Only recently have I found the self-confidence to make music with my children. I used to feel like I was so often on the sidelines—watching my husband play the guitar or piano. Now I play along with my kids. What joy! For years I longed for something of my own—something that was only mine. It seemed like there was no time for me to have an avocation. Now that I'm on my own, I'm discovering a sense of my own powers. I used to be unable to swim, now I scuba dive. When I was married, I was afraid to try anything new. Now I'm willing to try anything. I think I'm much more aware of my children's potential now that I'm a single mother. I used to be under the influence of my husband's judgmental attitude so it was more difficult for me to accept my children's individuality. Now I'm so much more open with myself and my children.

I was sixteen when I got married and had a baby soon after that. Seemed like I had four before I knew it. I always lived in the country. I think you got a better chance raising kids there than in the city. I stayed home with them until they were old enough to stay in the house by themselves. My oldest began to watch the little ones and I started getting work again. I don't pay anyone to watch my kids. We don't make that much, but we get by. The most important thing I do in this world is teach my kids right from wrong. I take my little girl with me when I do housework for people. She's been watchin' me clean for some time now. When she helps me, I make her go back over it if it's not right. Now she's got a job of her own on Friday evenings.

Raising kids is nothing really if you've got the money to do it. It's hard with four. Sometimes you just have to tell them that you just don't have the money to get it. I'm not complaining, though. When my boys and girls are out of the house, it sounds like a dead house. When they're back from school, it sounds like it's alive again. Little children are all born alike. It's up to the mother to train them. If you pull your kids together, they're going to stay. If you don't, they're not. That's a woman's job, to keep her family together. My own mother taught me that. She died when I was thirteen, but I miss her today.

My sister's baby boy just up and died in the night for no reason. She laid him down to sleep and he just stopped breathing. She completely broke down and has never recovered. Having a child can certainly change you for the better or worse. I used to be pretty wild and on-the-go, but since I had my kids, I just want to stay at home. I think I was always lookin' for something, and then when I had a baby, I felt like I'd found it. I feel calmer and better about myself. When my sister comes to visit, she picks up my babies and cries. I know having another child would make her feel better about herself but she's so afraid of getting hurt again. Her loss makes me more protective of my own children. Whenever I wake up in the night, I'll go check my kids' breathing. Sometimes I act real silly and pat 'em to make sure they'll move. To lose a child is a woman's greatest fear. I dread it more than my own death.

I know I have to go out of the house and work because we need the money to raise them. I feel grateful to have a job so I can buy them the things they want. It does me good to get out of the house too. I appreciate them more when I get home at the end of the day. I feel lucky that I can leave my kids with my own mother, so they spend the day with someone who loves them. She wouldn't stand for anyone else to watch them. We wouldn't let my grandmother go to a nursing home. She died in her bed at home, with her children and grandchildren around her. A woman's most important job is to hold the family together. I plan on watching my own grandchildren one day. We are a family that pulls together. Nothing can separate us.

It was important to me to have a home and be established (professionally) before I had a child. It's strange how quickly memories of her babyhood disappear after only six years. I always used to photograph her when she was really small and changing all the time. My husband and I raise and train race horses on our farm. We are lucky that we both work together at home and she's easily become a part of our life. We take her everywhere with us. It's a lot better for her and me that her daddy's around on the farm during the day.

She seems so perfect to us, I think we've never felt a need to have another. In the horse business you have to travel a lot and you couldn't drag two or three children around everywhere with you. But with one, you can. The three of us make a family that seems complete. Because my husband was around the house when she was a baby, he always knew what hard work raising a little child is. I think that since both of us work with animals all day, we're used to being in charge of helpless creatures. Living on a farm makes you more accepting of the natural course of things.

I felt totally unprepared for my first child. I had never been around small babies before. The pregnancy itself was a surprise. Even though we were newlyweds and still adapting to being married, being pregnant made us feel like a couple. I was twenty-four at the time and we had an instant family. When the baby was only twelve months I got pregnant again. Because we were young, we played a lot with our children. We took them around everywhere. The third child really slows you down. It's harder to do so many things outside the house with three. I guess I just got tired. I got a little depressed after the third child because I did feel stuck in the house, really for the first time. I felt like I was losing myself, because it seemed the children's demands on my time were never-ending. Now my youngest is growing up so fast, I wish she'd slow down.

I do many things the way my parents did. I believe in the old school of discipline because it always worked. I always wanted to have my kids before I was thirty, to enjoy them while I was still young. It wasn't until I was married and had children of my own that I saw a real friend in my mother. I want my children to feel I'm more accessible, that they can talk to me about anything when they need to. I've done it all before so I'm not afraid of what my children might do, especially when they get older. My own mother didn't want to know everything about me when I was a teenager. I think our generation is more relaxed than our parents', more willing to talk. We have different expectations for our kids. We're more concerned with the interior success than the outward success of our children. I feel I'll be able to give helpful guidance because I won't be shocked. I rely on my husband a lot when it comes to decision and policy making. I can't imagine how single mothers raise small children by themselves. I know it's not impossible, but it must be harder not having a caring husband around. It's been a long nine years, always having a child at home. This will be the first time I've had time alone in nine years. I have mixed feelings about all three of them out of the house all day.

I'm surprised how much I enjoy being a housewife and mother. I'm glad I don't have to have a job; life is hectic enough as is. I've never been the cheerleading type, but I get really caught up in the boys' Little League. I really like the work of being a mom, and I appreciate the moments in the day when I don't have to answer to anyone.

I was twenty-nine and just starting to take myself, and my work as a photographer, seriously when I first got pregnant. I can't say it was completely an accident because I think it was an unconsciously wanted pregnancy. Some part of me wanted a child; but I think I made a very rational decision that it would be unwise to become a mother at that time in my life—not only for me, but, obviously, for the child. My lover was someone I couldn't marry; and I guess I always thought that being a parent was a big job—and I knew I wasn't ready to do it well.

When I learned I was pregnant, it was good news to know that I could conceive. It was important information about my life, and I was glad to have that information, even though I wasn't ready to put it to use yet. At that time, I was changing a lot of my ideas about what I should do and what I had to do as a woman and as a person. I was establishing the kind of person I'd be for the rest of my life. Those changes have a lot to do with what I think makes me a good parent today. My work is an important part of who I am. It's not a priority over motherhood for my life, but it was the priority for those years of my life.

My family very much disapproved of my publicly "admitting" that I'd had an abortion, but I felt it was important for women not to be secretive so that other women know they're not alone. There was a myth that only "bad" women had abortions. So "proper" women never told—and the myth was enlarged. I was so grateful to have that choice. I've always felt I made the right choice for me at that time, and I've never regretted not having a child then.

I have a feeling that a lot of the anti-abortion movement is really antisexual. It's as if "bad" girls should be punished. I don't think marriage legitimizes sex and I don't think women should be forced by law to choose between asexual lives and motherhood.

Five years after the abortion, I had a very much wanted child with a man who was committed to raising the child with me. I was enormously curious about the experience of motherhood; but I had no idea how fascinating an infant could be—both emotionally and intellectually. I think mothering is the most exciting, moving thing I've done in my life.

My life right now is definitely a challenge. Everyone knows about the demands of a two-year-old, and my daughter is a very complex person. I find I really have to stretch myself to meet her. I often see myself in her. Nothing is simple or easy—but she is also delightful. She is very sensitive and I suppose I was like that too. Life is easier for me now that I'm an adult. I spent most of my years trying to control things, but I've come to realize that perfection is a self-defeating goal. I can now embrace life with all its imperfections and it makes my days easier—a lot more fun. This is one of the most valuable lessons my love for my children has taught me.

The whole time I was carrying my son, I knew it was a male baby and I was apprehensive about it. I feel so completely able to relate to my daughter and I was afraid I couldn't be as close to a boy. Having a son has made me feel a lot more compassionate toward men. It has closed the gap. I think I was a little bit afraid, even angry, with men before I had a son. I know it sounds simple, but it took me a long time to figure out the similar humanity in males and females. I needed a son to learn that lesson. My children have opened my heart and helped me grow up.

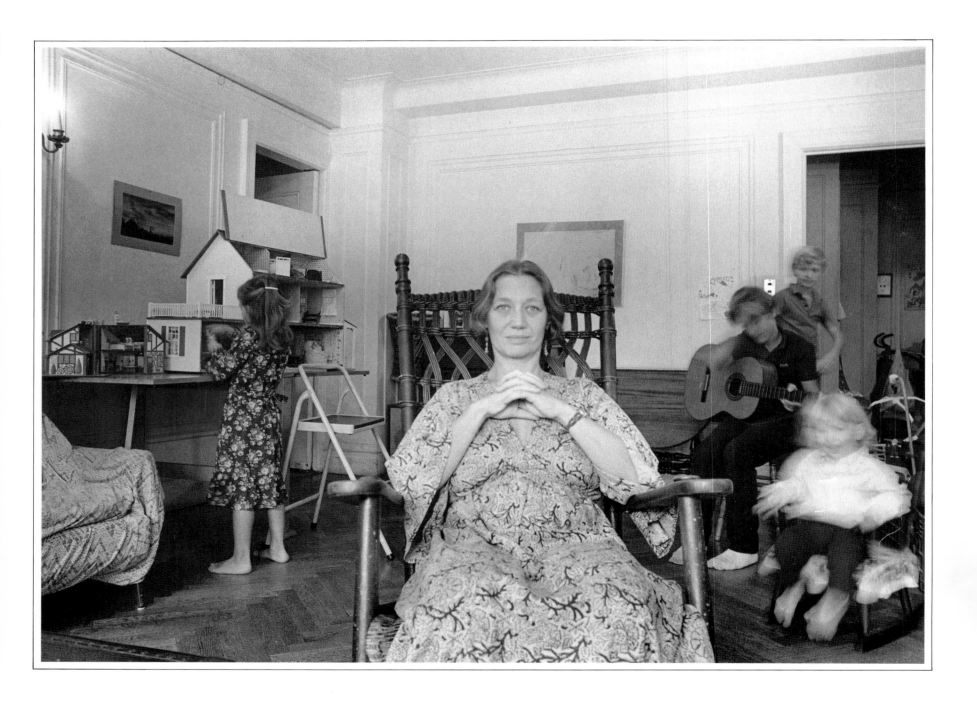

I have four small children and live in New York City. It's not reasonable, but it's what I want to do. I never thought I wanted a large family. I was thirty-one when I had my oldest son. I was so scared. I wasn't sure I wanted to have a child. I was at a low point in my career in dance and after seven years of marriage we thought we'd have a child. I loved my new shape. I learned so much about myself during that time. Someone gave me a bag of baby clothes. I took one look and thought, "Oh, my God!" I put them away and didn't look at them again. I loved my belly, but I wasn't so sure I wanted a baby. On the delivery table, when my doctor told me to push, I thought, "I don't want a baby." We had no preparation at all for the reality of raising a child. I was frightened. I sobbed the whole way home from the hospital. I'd never cried in front of my husband. I didn't know how I'd cope. Soon the love took over and I quickly had four children. I never felt so fulfilled. Of course, there's not much applause, but the gratification that comes from the special relationship with each child makes all the work worthwhile.

I continued working and dancing after my first child was born, but with each child I've stayed home more and more. It feels right to me to be comfortable with the fact that life is change. I was dancing, now I spend my time with four children, and eventually my days will be filled with something else. The biggest challenge and frustration was trying to do both dance and mothering. I came to the realization that I didn't have to keep myself in one image. My life is now coming together. I feel less divided, my interest in dance has evolved into an interest in infant movement. I've become a childbirth educator and a body therapist. I used to feel so pulled apart when I tried to keep my old identity and take on the new one of mother. I feel much more centered now, free of the different incompatible roles I had to perform daily. With each child, it's better. I enjoy the experience of watching them grow. My children have really taught me what's important, how to slow down. I hold classes in my home for pregnant and postpartum families and no longer work outside the home. There is some loss of status and prestige when you no longer work in the marketplace. Raising a family is not as respected as it should be. It's vital, important work. My respect in the community comes more from being a childbirth educator than from raising my four children. If you don't make money, you're powerless, and if you're powerless, you get no respect. My own mother doesn't understand my life-style. Our homes are completely different; yet every time I open my mouth, I can hear her voice.

I didn't get married until I was thirty-one and didn't get around to thinking about having babies for several years after that. Eventually it seemed to be the right time but I never got pregnant. We did the fertility doctor bit and it was humiliating and infuriating. Their attitude toward me was outrageous. They left you waiting for hours and treated you like a piece of meat. I never went through the complete battery of tests because we realized what we really wanted was a family. We weren't that hung up on having biological children of our own. Adoption seemed like a natural next step for us. At the same time, we had two inner-city children staying with us for the summer. We took them in, frequently, for seven years, and they taught me that it is possible to love any child you're responsible for. Of course, I would have liked to have had the experience of being pregnant, but it's hard to imagine the love for an adoptive child as any less than that for your own baby. We really wanted to adopt these two boys when their mother died, but their grandmother wouldn't permit it. It was quite a blow, but the experience with them made us more than ready to adopt a child.

We went to a state agency where there is a book of photographs of children who are available for adoption. It's a strange feeling to flip through a catalogue for a child. We wanted a girl because we felt it was too soon for our hearts to try to replace the two boys who we had first tried to adopt. The little girl we adopted had been given up by her own mother at birth and placed with a family who turned out to be abusive, then placed back in foster homes. We got her at sixteen months. Already it was hard for her to trust. Seven months later we adopted our little boy, who was almost three. He, too, had been badly abused. It's taken him years to really relax and be trusting. He was resistant to physical affection for years. He used to flinch every time he spilled his milk. He was terrified when the caseworkers came around that he'd be taken away from us. These kids had lived through a child's worst fear—being separated from those who love you. Those first few years I felt like they were often testing my love. What's hard to accept at first is that adoption is often a time of grief for the child, even though it's a joyful time for the adoptive parents. They've lost everything familiar and are understandably distrustful of a new situation. Somehow it never occurred to us that our love wouldn't win their trust. To see them come out of their shells and love us back was and is a wonderful privilege. They had to learn to love me. As a result, we are so grateful for our mutual trust and affection. When you adopt, your kids are not an accident. They are truly wanted children and we had to patiently wait for them to be able to love us. After the novelty and excitement of having a new child wears off, the enormity of the act of adoption suddenly hits you like a ton of bricks. Before you know it, they've got a strong foothold in your heart and

a family begins. That's when the real beauty of love starts.

I miss two things: the ego trip of seeing what a new shake-up of your family's genes will do and the experience of physically bearing a child. But I can't think of my children as "someone else's"—I'm their mother. When my kid gets angry at me and says, "You're not my real mother," I say, "Yes, I am. I adopted you—that makes me your real mother."

Because we're immigrants, everything we accomplished had to be dug out of our own flesh. Also, whatever emotional and psychological support is given to our young children has to come from us alone because there is no safety net of an extended family of relatives. I'm glad I didn't put off starting a family until I was older because I now realize how we lose our adaptability as we grow older. We lose a lot of our foolhardy optimism as we age. I don't understand the concept of "quality time" with small children. If you leave your baby eight hours a day and then return to him, he will eventually not need you because you've forced him to learn to do without.

I don't feel like mothering is a one-way street. It seems like many women I know see the job as all take and no give. For me, my relationship with my children has given me a second chance to learn lessons about our own humanity. My two little ones have taught me things that I missed with my own mother. One of the basic emotional symmetries of life is the mother-child relationship. The love that you get as a child and give as an adult in this bond makes you a whole person. I feel much more complete as a person since my children were born. My relationship with my son and daughter has taught me to communicate more freely than I ever knew possible.

For me, a marriage without children wouldn't have much meaning. The connection I feel for my son and daughter has taught me to feel close to my husband. My own childhood was not very emotionally fulfilling. I was a lonely only child. I feel like my husband and my children have given me a second chance to find happiness. I'm not a religious person. I have no belief in life after death; yet my children give me a sense of immortality. I find comfort in the fact that my biological and cultural inheritance will live on in them. I don't know how I could bear my own mortality if I hadn't become a mother. The meaning of life is survival; so in that sense, having children gives life meaning. It changes a finite life span into an open-ended process. I will love being a grandmother. Life is so beautifully strange. My mother always wanted to leave Hungary and come to the United States. She never made it, but here I am. Each generation is another small step in evolution.

We're going through hard times right now. I feel like every time I get up on my feet, there's something there to knock me right back down. I've been trying very hard to get a job for a long time (since I was sacked). My twins just can't empathize with the frustration of my efforts. The little that I make, they spend it all. Their first eight years we lived the good life. Since my divorce it's been hard for them to realize that we are no longer affluent. The three of us living in two rooms is difficult for all of us. I feel closed in. They are mirror twins. One is left-sided and one is right. A reflection of each other; there are two of them and one of me. Both are as hot tempered and high-strung as I am. Not an easy situation.

Twenty years ago I was burning up the world. I've always been ambitious. I still am, but now I can't gamble. The loss of money and living space means nothing to me compared to being unable to find meaningful work. At the height of my career in fashion design, I was making more money than my husband. I left New York to follow my husband to Europe and now, after so many years, it's impossible to get back in the business again. No one remembers me. It's difficult to start a career all over again at my age. The longer you're out of the job market, the harder it is to get work. If you're desperate for a job they don't want you. I'm a dreamer, an artist. I really have no marketable skills other than fashion design. It's hard to talk about myself. It hurts. I don't even feel like myself anymore. Fear of losing everything kept me in my marriage for so long. I knew this would happen. My girls blame me for our hardship.

As far as mothering my daughters now that they're almost eighteen—I lay the ground rules and nobody listens. None of us is terribly domestic. Sometimes I think they feel I'm a failure. My relationship with my children is one of extremes. Sometimes I feel very close to them. At other times, we're like strangers. It's a thankless job. I gave everything I had to give to them. They are a part of me and I love them. Maybe I don't really know what love is all about. I'm so consumed by all the hurt and sucked into the hopelessness. My daughters are special young women. Both of my girls have great potential for success. They are going to go on to do great things because I've socked everything I have, everything I've got to give, into them. There's nothing left of me. I'm just a shell, an empty shell.

When I walked down the aisle, I knew my husband and I wanted a large family. Six children later I still have my faith in the Catholic Church and the institution of marriage, but my husband feels trapped and is leaving us. Since he's totally committed to leaving, there's no need for me to dwell on the past. I like to make plans for the future. I don't want to lose my marriage, but if I have to I'll make the best of it. In a strange way, my life will be easier now than it was when my children were younger. My husband worked day and night, and there were times when it was impossible for me to even get out of the house because I had so many little kids. He escaped the stresses of family life through his work. He's always kept his distance with the children as well as with me. The chaos of a large family was insurmountable to him. Since I did most all the work of raising the children anyway, the biggest change in my life after he leaves will be that I won't have to consider my husband's wishes when I make decisions.

I have lots of plans for the future. I'd like to go into water sculptures and landscaping. It's been a dream of mine for a long time. I'm taking courses in small business and sculpture. My little girl has one more year at home before school, so I won't change into this full-time until she's out of the house all day. I stayed home to raise my kids and I wouldn't have it any other way. Not that it was easy having so many little toddlers home at once. I had to put my creative side on the shelf for quite some time. My sanity was saved by the fact that my sister lived nearby. We let the housework go and the children scramble around on the kitchen floor while we drank coffee and designed a passive solar house. We poured so much energy and imagination into those house plans. I really wanted to live in that house, but we never had it built. My husband never really had confidence in the plans that he was not actively involved in.

After my fountain and landscape business is established, I still plan on building my dream house. It will be a live-in sculpture. Life is as much your attitude about what happens to you as what actually happens to you. The secret to happiness is appreciating what we do have. Six healthy children is something to be grateful for.

I grew up in the Dominican Republic. I was married so long ago, I can hardly remember. I had my first child at sixteen. We married for love and it never occurred to me to use birth control, for our religion considered it a sin. Because of the Catholic Church, large families were common. Children were considered a blessing. I wasn't afraid of being pregnant—it made me proud and happy, but I was totally innocent in these matters. I didn't really understand how babies were made. I had no idea how you gave birth to a child. Here I was, in labor, and I had no idea how the baby was going to get out. My own mother was with me along with the doctor, at home. I probably would have been even more scared if I had been alone in the hospital. At least women here know a little bit of what to expect in labor. Much of my pain was fear, I'm sure. After my first child was born, I felt real comfortable with that little baby. I took a lot of pleasure in caring for it. A year later, I had another one. I think it's a nice custom for the husband to be with the mother during childbirth. My children's father was always behind a closed door. We did as the Church and our parents expected of us. Traditions of our culture and religion made our decisions for us. A teenager grows up fast with several children. By the time I was twenty-nine I had six kids. I think my husband was proud to have a large family, but it was real hard on me. I nearly died having the last one and I was overwhelmed by the burden of so many children.

It was impossible for us to make any money in the Dominican Republic when my children were small. Our financial situation eventually got so bad that I had to come to the United States in order to support the family. Even though we were poorer there than we are here now, I'm not sure that our life is any better. In many ways we're worse off than before. My husband and I left the children behind to come to the States to find work and then sent for them as soon as we could. It took me almost three years to get them here. It was a living hell. I was sending them money but they weren't getting it. My children were practically starved while I was away from them. They eventually got here one at a time. They always understood that I left them to try and make a better life. It was a happy day when I had all six of them back together with me again. For years I cried every day. It's a terrible feeling to have to leave your kids behind, but I have no regrets about being here. The children are beginning to speak English very well, and though I can't speak it yet I can understand a lot. I do a lot of babysitting for working mothers while my children are in school. I usually have between five and eight other children here to watch over. The pay is no good, but it's something I can do when my English is not very good. It's something I'm good at. Children always like me.

I need to learn English so I can speak to my grandchildren one day. I only hope that my children

don't have as many children as I did. It's just too hard. Two is enough. It's too frustrating to not be able to buy them the things they want. The miracle is that you can love six babies as much as you love one. The love comes with the child. As the love grows, so does the worry. I can't sleep until I know they're all safe inside the apartment. There is so much fear in the life on the streets here. A mother's love and fear are never-ending.

I got married after college and had a child because it never occurred to me to do anything else. I went to a good college, but never really had any career expectations. I really enjoyed staying home with a small baby. I never got lonely because I enjoyed my son's company. He had a good sense of humor. It was a good period for me. I think the nursing kept my frequent depressions at bay. Until I was on antidepressants, I never had a longer space of time without a major funk. When I had to go back to work, I started to have problems with motherhood. I missed that feeling of being in touch with my child. Information was secondhand as opposed to observing myself. I felt more content when I didn't have to always be coming and going. A stay-at-home mother has a shock when she tries to reenter the work force. It's not waiting with open arms. Economic necessity was my sole motivation for working outside the home. My husband and I tried so hard to make our marriage work, but we couldn't give each other the emotional support we needed. Finally separation was a necessity, but life wasn't much easier raising a child alone.

My closest woman friend started to get involved with my son's problems that stemmed from the recent divorce. I was so grateful to have the support she offered. She needed a connection with the next generation and my son thrived under her attentions. When I came down with the flu, she took me home with her. Her husband became equally close to my son and myself. Pretty soon it became obvious that we were all better off together emotionally and financially than we were apart. We were comfortable as a family and felt stronger when we pooled our resources. My son was a very angry child until he got the additional caring of them both. My own mother even sees how wonderful it is for us to have the support of two committed adults.

Quite often they are able to be closer to my son than I am. In a way, it's like having three parents. I no longer have this sinking sense of my child and myself against the world. I feel stronger from the protection of their commitment to us. I don't think children are supposed to be raised one on one. I was raised by a single mother, since my father died when I was six. It was hard on her, and us as well. Both my brother and I are still struggling to catch up emotionally from that sense of loss. All three of us could have used more committed loving care during my childhood. If no man is an island, it's even more difficult for a woman to be totally responsible for her child's well-being. The responsibility is staggering without any outside help.

Even though I'm not in any position to have another child at this point, I'm still susceptible to "baby hunger." Especially as I get older, each time I have a period it reminds me that there's one less month left to satisfy that hunger. When I was young, I never paid much attention to my monthly cycles, but now I'm aware of their finiteness and they are

much more precious to me. I feel my fertility passing. I couldn't bring myself to have my tubes tied.

The permanence scares me, yet birth control is terrible. Mother Nature really has it rigged.

Raising my daughters in New York City makes them more independent. They are aware of more issues, less sheltered. They do live in a frightening world and in the city there is no way to protect them from that fact.

I've always trusted my intuition, my physical feelings. We feel real comfortable together. I love the feeling of closeness. Just to lie on the bed and giggle and talk. I think it's important to keep that family feeling of togetherness. I think it's the best. In my life, it's given me the most happiness. Sometimes I feel so content, I think I must be really simplistic. Giving birth, the whole process of nurturing has been so satisfying. I've never felt like I sacrificed my work for my children. I felt I wanted to be there, and now I'm glad because I realize how brief those years are. They are only children once, yet I think it's good for children to see their mothers take on different roles. I feel I've been lucky because I had plenty of opportunity to preserve time for myself, to satisfy needs outside of my nurturing. Sometimes I look at my girls and I'd like to freeze time. It's so fleeting. Watching my children grow up helps me appreciate my life. You get to see the process. It's almost like being born again. You get the depth of reliving your own life experiences again. Even though connection is important to me, I'm awed by how separate we are from our children. Everyone has to take their own journey. The hardest part of motherhood is watching them suffer, not being able to protect them from pain. It's important to be on your child's side. Even though you can't live their life for them, you can be there for them if they need you.

I feel like I'm flowing along the river of my life, passive and receptive. I admire people who really take charge of their lives. I feel I'm becoming more assertive, but it doesn't come naturally for me. I want my daughters to have work they can call their own.

I got pregnant right after I got married. I was ready to have a baby. I'm amazed every day how big my kids are growing. Tears well up in my eyes. I can't believe it's all gone. It's not that I want a baby again, but it really measures your age. I never think of my age, but other people often perceive you by your biological age. Now that I'm forty, it's scary to think that in a couple of years my options for having a baby will be closed. It's hard to think of myself as too old to do something. I've loved every part of watching my daughter and son go through so many changes.

I remember how strong my feelings were when I was young. Growing up, I had a friend whose mother always seemed so interested in me. I vowed that when I had kids I'd be like her. To this day I remind myself to be less involved in myself and be more like my friend's mother. I try to keep up on music and trends so I can feel a part of them, not just some "old person" who's "out of it." They are very curious about any secrets going on in my life. I have to respect their privacy too, yet I like them to feel like they can open up around me if they want to. It's hard being divorced because you can never really be a replacement for their father. They are very interested in my male friends. Sometimes they even feel threatened by my boyfriends. My son likes me to be the helpless female so he can be the man around the house, and my daughter tends to compare me to her father—something I doubt she'd do so much if we didn't keep separate households.

I guess I always assumed I'd be a mother. Yet even now, when I look at my thirteen-year-old daughter and think back on her as a baby, I think, "Okay, now I get it. This is what it's like to have a child! She's mine." Sometimes, though, I call her my younger sister's name because I still don't think of myself as a grown-up. In my head I don't feel any different than I was at sixteen. I don't think I'll ever feel like The Mother. I keep waiting for that age. I can remember making my own mother cry by saying some cruel remark about her body when she was about my age. I was just shocked that she was so sensitive. I don't really remember my mother in my daily life. Most of my memories are from home movies and snapshots. She was simply always there. I never thought of her as an individual. I don't think a child wants to know her mother intimately. It's too much of a burden. When children are young, they need their mother to be a figure of strength. I never wanted to be my mother's best friend, and I think it's a mistake to try. I, too, simply want to be there, available if they need me.

I was barely nineteen when I had my first child. There was always a longing to start my own family. When I was seventeen, I was pushed out of the nest on my own, so I got married young. My own parents shut the door on me once I was considered "grown," but I don't ever want to lose the sense of a heart network with my children. I want to be with them when they have children of their own and share family holidays and traditions together. There is a sense of sisterhood that I have with my girls. There is a common background of shared experience that you can't have with a son.

I feel closer to my children than even to my husband. The love never goes away, even in anger and frustration. I feel a powerful responsibility toward them. I experience their pain and their joy. I think of myself as a guide. When they ask me questions, I often anguish over the answers. In my work as a marriage counselor, I realize the importance of words as well as example, so I strive to be as articulate with my children as I can be. When my youngest was about two years old, I was doing some yoga exercises. I saw her doing the exact same thing, and it made me see what role models we are for our children. I'm very conscious of both my words and deeds, because I'm aware that, on some level, my children are watching me.

Our relationship with our children is a microcosm of God's relationship with us. The love we have for them gets us in touch with Him. Newborns seem almost God-like, full of clarity. Soon the husks grow over that fresh kernel of ourselves, and we spend a great portion of our lives trying to peel through the layers, back to our original selves. Children are much more in touch with magic, with the wonder of it all. The husks are our will or ego and we have to learn to let go to remove them to get back to the truth.

In family therapy, I see so often how our mothers are strangers to us. If we take away the role of mother, the women themselves are a mystery. My own mother took her own life ten years ago, and I don't really know why. I suspect it was because she never was able to develop her own sense of self. I want my own children to know me as a whole person, not just Mother. The richness of life springs from an appreciation of the many facets of who we are. I think if I only exposed the "mother" part of me to my children, I would be giving them an incomplete role model. I want to pass on to my children the ability to really develop themselves.

There's magic in the world. We're sometimes like the color-blind in a garden. Children have given me permission to discover.

Even though I'm a lawyer, I always knew that somewhere down the road I wanted children. Two seemed like the right number and I got pregnant right away both times I tried to conceive. I found that I loved doing child care so much that I cut back on my practice much more than I had planned. Since I was very much involved in the women's movement, I had to spend a lot of time defending my position. Many of my feminist friends felt I had betrayed them because I liked going to the playground. I think feminism means having choices. I did exactly what I wanted to. Their father shared a lot of the workload around the house. He would have probably done more, but I didn't want to leave my kids. When their dad took them to work, people thought it was wonderful to see such an involved, caring father. When I did the same thing, however, my colleagues were less than supportive. I felt pressure all around me to choose between being a lawyer and being a mother. I'm glad I didn't quit working completely because I want my daughters to have a role model of a mother who had interests outside the home.

Three years ago I discovered I had cancer. I had a breast removed and things looked pretty good for a while. My own mother died a year before from cancer. Just as I was back on my feet again, doctors discovered a lot of cancer in my lungs. I had to undergo chemotherapy, so for the second time I cut back on my law practice so I could rest at home. I lost all my hair and was very weak, but I never ever felt like giving up. I have two little kids and don't have time to die. A year ago the cancer went to my brain and I had to undergo radiation as well as chemotherapy. This time I lost interest in my law practice. I was losing patience with my clients. This disease really makes you evaluate your priorities. The thing I feel really good about is my mothering. Even though I'm less patient now because of my own anxiety, I've always loved my girls one hundred percent. They've grown up with two parents who have enjoyed them so much—and it shows. I know they have a lot to deal with right now. It's very frightening and it's hard for young children to express their feelings. When I think about the possibility of my children growing up without me, I vacillate between the terror that they won't manage and the horror that they'll do fine without me.

I was born in 1924 in Romania and lived there until I was a grown woman. I loved my own mother like my own life. When my parents were in the concentration camps during the war, I felt as if they died; I didn't want to live. When my husband took me to the United States, I was not so happy because I had to leave my mother. I never wanted children because I lived only for my mother. When my daughter was born, everything changed for me. I always worked outside the home until I was five months pregnant. Then my husband said, "From now on this child is your job." To this day I feel this way. Perhaps she is a spoiled child, I don't know. My daughter says I never let her alone. Even when she's in school, I worry for her. Now that my mother has died, she is my whole life. I think the love I had for my own mother and for my daughter is the same love. I was forty-three when my daughter was born. I didn't want a child. I was too old, but thank God I had her. It made me feel young. I spent all my time with her. She never went anywhere alone until she was twelve or thirteen years old. I hope I live to be a grandmother someday. One of my main pleasures in life is watching my daughter grow. I haven't forgotten what it's like to be young. I remember so well being my daughter's age. I still feel the same way inside as I did then. When I look in the mirror and see my wrinkles, I can't believe it.

Before my child was born, I was really afraid I wouldn't know how to take care of her. I don't know any other way except to give love. I was so nervous when she was little, for five months I had a friend bathe her, my hands were shaking so. Every time she wasn't hungry, I'd worry. Now when she's outside of the house, my mind is always thinking, where is she, what's she doing? She is very independent. My love has given her the freedom to stand by herself.

I was married at nineteen, and a mother by twenty. Those days [the 1950s] were different. You were innocent. I don't think I even knew about birth control. I never planned my children—they happened. I never planned out my life. I just assumed my husband would take care of me. By the time I was twenty-four, I had three children under three. It was fun. I felt proud of them. I wasn't exposed to a lot of options growing up. I didn't have any expectations to do anything but raise my children at that time. My fourth and last child was an altogether different experience because I was older and more appreciative and grateful. It seems I'm still the mother. I'm still cooking and washing twenty-eight years later. I'm doing the best I can, but I suffer guilt. I'm feeling guilty about everything all the time. I still take responsibility for my children's happiness. I would feel guilty if I got sick. I run a small business with my kids, but I still can't think of myself as a career woman. Our family is like a team. We sometimes wonder why we have to have each other's approval. I think it keeps us from getting enough accomplished and then I feel guilty about that. Maybe the guilt is necessary to drive us through the work to be done, or maybe it's just caring.

I never raised my children with any particular mold in mind. My whole thing was, if they feel good about themselves—that's all I care about. If they're miserable—I feel as terrible for them as I did when they were babies.

I always knew I was adopted, even long before I really knew what that meant. As a very young child, I think I was very proud of the fact. When I got to my teens, I had a great deal of curiosity about my birth mother, yet I felt very guilty about that curiosity. After I had my own two children, I finally got nerve to ask my mother if she knew about my biological parents. She denied that she had any information, but years later she changed her mind and sent me my birth certificate. She was very jealous of my birth mother. In fact, after I was born, my biological parents asked for a picture of me and my adoptive mom sent her a picture of an unattractive male cousin. She was so afraid that I'd be taken back from her.

Being an only child, and an adopted child, I longed for the physical intimacy of my own babies. It's wonderful to have the total trust of that unconditional love. That thread between us is invaluable to me. Until I had my own boys, I never felt like I really belonged. I felt outside of the family circle. Now I feel like I'll never be completely alone. My sons are always in the background. It's difficult to talk about the loving. It's so precious to you, you're afraid you'll lose it if you let it out in the open.

My kids are twenty-one and nineteen now, but I still feel they're the most important thing I've done in my life. They don't need mothering anymore now. They only need to feel my approval of their independence. I need their approval of mine, also. For the first time in my life, most of my concerns are mainly about my needs instead of others.

Growing up in the country in Korea, it was almost impossible to get an education or make much money. My family worked the land and it was hard to support a family. After I was married and had two children, we had a hard time supporting ourselves. I wanted a better life for them than I had myself. Education is the most important thing because it's something no one can take away from you. We decided to come to the United States to give our children a better life. My own mother was very sad to see us go. It is hard. I haven't seen her now for ten years. It is my hope one day to have my parents live here in the U.S. with me. My husband still misses Korea and thinks of going back one day; but me, I don't know. I don't think my children would want to live anywhere else but here. They are American now.

Living here has given my children an opportunity for art and piano lessons. My daughter will go to college next year. My son does very well in school, but he thinks he wants to go out into the world and make money instead of going to college. I hope he will change his mind, then he won't have to work as hard as his father and I do. We've worked for many, many years twelve hours a day without a vacation. My kids help with the cooking and cleaning at home since they have more time than we do.

I think each generation should be a little better off than the one before. I can work so hard because I'm giving my children a chance to have more choices in life. My main desire is that my children have a good education. Then one day I'd like to see them have children of their own.

I've had to work hard at the fruit store six days a week since we came to this country. I lived near work so I could keep an eye on my kids when they were home from school. Here women are too busy to help each other because they work and raise kids. Korean women have more time to help their neighbors because they don't have jobs outside the home. I've had to get used to doing everything myself with no help from friends. Many families are too busy for each other. The children grow up and leave the parents' house and have their own lives. It's not expected that the grandparents help raise their grandchildren. Everyone (even the parents in their old age) is on his own. It's strange to me that the old have no respect here. I think children should give their parents more respect. How could anyone let their mother die alone? Americans seem to teach their children to care about themselves first before others. I try to teach my kids to have a sense of responsibility for others as well as themselves.

I wasn't really trained for a career. My ultimate goal was getting married, even though I enjoyed my jobs and being single in my early twenties. When I got married, I quit working and moved to the suburbs to be a full-time wife. After being a gadabout, I felt like a prisoner stuck in my house away from the city. I was lonely; I just assumed we'd have children, so I was crushed when my husband said he didn't want any. He'd been married before and had two kids with his first wife and didn't want any more. It's unbelievable to me now that we'd never discussed having children before we were married. He just assumed I'd take care of his children during the summer. I kept longing for children of my own, but it was hard for us to communicate. We were both products of our generation. We both had our own assumptions, but couldn't share them with each other. When I got pregnant anyway, I was delighted, but he left me. He felt betrayed. Instead of things getting better, they got worse. I had to ask him to come see our daughter after she was born. I kept hoping he'd come back, but he never did until I asked for a divorce. That seemed to get his attention when he thought he might really lose me. I always felt like he wanted to own me.

After a while I got pregnant again. He was much more accepting of the second pregnancy. I loved taking care of the children. Teaching them and watching them grow was a great pleasure for me at that time. Even though my marriage was not very close, my relationship with my daughter and my son was warm and loving.

One summer when the children were older and off at camp, I became totally infatuated with my hairdresser. Something woke up in me that had been sleeping for fifteen years. I followed him to the West Coast. I was a desperate person. I was running for my life. My husband changed the locks and got an unlisted phone number. I knew he wouldn't let me see my children if I left him. It was a terrible price to pay, but I had to do it. It would have been worse for them if I had dragged them away from their schools and friends. I figured they'd be better off with their dad because he had money and position in society. I didn't know what the hell was going to happen to me. I knew he'd give them a good education. I lost contact with my whole world. I missed the children so much, it defies description. I felt very guilty. When my new relationship fell apart, I felt like I deserved it. It was over a year before I was able to see my children. I realized I couldn't even live near my children if I was to be free of my husband's domination. I made a whole new life for myself thousands of miles away. My work means a lot to me now, but it took me many years to patch up the pieces of my life.

In many ways, my relationship with my children now that they're grown is very open because nothing shocks me or them. We've worked hard to rebuild our relationship, and we appreciate each

other more as a result. I'm able to be friends with my daughter, since she certainly doesn't place me on a pedestal. I tell her I took the low road to finding meaning in life.

Eagles learn to fly by falling out of the nest. They don't know if they are ready to fly until they fall. That's how my children grew up. They are terrific.

MOTHER: When I was raising my five children thirty years ago, birth control was not very reliable and we therefore had a lot less control over our own lives. Also, men were just returning from World War II and they wanted their jobs back. Women were supposed to stay at home and the community was supportive of large families. If a woman didn't get married and have children, she was considered odd. A career as a doctor was unusual for a mother. My generation didn't question the status quo. We sought it out. I was through medical school and in general practice when I had my first child—ten months after I got married. For the first three months, I continued to work and I was considered an exception to the rule. We moved because of my husband's practice. I found myself pregnant again. I had a third child a year after the second, so there I was, a doctor, staying at home with three small children. It would have practically been unthinkable to do otherwise back then. I can remember making angel wings at the church bazaar and thinking, "How did my life take such a turn?" Of course, my feelings for the children, the overriding sense of responsibility I had for them, overcame the frustration of not being able to practice medicine in the early years of motherhood. An M.D. doesn't change your relationship with your child. You're *it.*

DAUGHTER: When I had my first child in the 1980s, I had been running my own business for years and I wasn't prepared for the change in my self-image. I was depressed a month after my baby was born. People told me it was hormonal, "postpartum depression." I had to get rid of this image I had of an "ideal mother" and be more realistic. The thought of those long days alone at home for eighteen years scared me to death. I was afraid of losing my identity as a photographer. My mother has been very supportive of me not giving up the business I'd spent ten years building. She is my Medici!

MOTHER: It's such a terrifying revelation. You can't

know it until the baby's born. I felt that sense of despair from leaving behind years of medical school internship for full-time domestic life. I told my daughter, "You don't want to give up that studio." I know the feeling, and I don't think if a mother has outside support it is necessary. I had no one to help me care for my children or encourage me to continue my work. Women in the church told me, "You *must* stay home," as if it were written in stone. Back then a woman's status in the community was directly related to the number of children she had and her husband's job. In fact, you weren't supposed to be very smart, it wasn't "ladylike." You were proud to have a lot of children then, whereas now you'd have to be almost apologetic.

DAUGHTER: Now I think women are in the difficult position of being torn apart by society's messages. If you stay home with your children you're not given much respect, and if you leave your kids with someone else, you're looked down on as a "bad mother." Women are left alone with themselves to figure that one out. It's a very personal decision how you handle it. I've come to the realization that perfection is not a reasonable expectation, and I've learned to compromise and set priorities. I think the kids do okay in daycare centers, but the mothers don't, because they feel guilty that they aren't the television "good mom" always by the kitchen door with fresh-baked cookies.

MOTHER: We don't yet know the psychological impact on human development from being raised in daycare. This generation's children eventually will let us know.

DAUGHTER: Even if women are full-time wage earners, they are still expected to have most of the responsibility for their children and housework. There is not a moment in the day when I'm not aware of my daughter, even at work; yet I'm sure my husband's workday is not altered by the fact he has a child. We hear them cry in the night while our husbands are sleeping soundly. My child's sobs have a physical impact on me.

MOTHER: I stayed at home and had five children in ten years. I had to turn my mind away from medicine—block my past. It was too frustrating to look back. When my youngest was in second grade, I decided to go back and that was such an exhilarating time in my life. I found a whole new world had opened up. It was thrilling, I soaked in lectures and books. It was quite a different life after eighteen years of child raising. I practiced for a couple of years and decided to go back into residency in psychiatry at forty-eight years old. It was a lifelong dream of mine. My contemporaries were the staff, and here I was with all these young medical students. I feel my experience raising five children was a great asset in my residency. All that life experience was a great background for me. I'm thrilled with my private psychiatric practice and my emerging role of grandmother. I'm like a young doctor as opposed to someone my age because of my recent training.

DAUGHTER: I was in college when my mom resumed her profession. I thought it was great. Even though she has always given me great encouragement for my own photographic career, she is the same woman who warned me not to beat the guys in tennis. I feel like it's important for a woman to have earning power. It's too risky to remain financially dependent on a man. It's not responsible or realistic in this day and age when so many marriages break up. There's no way I feel like I could stay home for eighteen years and then go back to work.

MOTHER: I was fortunate that I already had an M.D. degree, yet I remember feeling frustrated that I couldn't get a Sears credit card because I had no income. I could only get a card in my husband's name. Now I'm proud of having my own credit rating. But I tell you one thing, you can talk about all the professions and graduate degrees you want, but there's nothing like motherhood. To have that baby is one of life's greatest pleasures. Being a grandmother is even better. You get all of the good parts without the drudgery. I love to see the changes that have taken place in my daughter since she has a daughter of her own. Although she's still a competent professional, she has become more well-rounded. She's taken a new interest in domesticity.

DAUGHTER: I think I also appreciate my work more. My ability to produce is more valued. I'm a lot more organized because I have to be. I don't have time to be unhappy. I no longer worry about my own personal fulfillment, because having a child makes you so other-directed. It takes you outside of yourself and your concerns are turned away from your own problems. Babies help you find yourself by losing yourself. I feel much more rounded than I ever have before. It teaches you to trust your instincts. I used to judge my own mother more harshly. Now that I'm a mother myself, I see how humans can do no more than their best and that I can't be perfect any more than she could.

MOTHER: We all fantasize a perfect mother. No one really has one. Everyone thinks they'll be better than their own mother.

DAUGHTER: It takes a while for the new identity of mother to sink in. I remember going into the camera store with my daughter and thinking, "Where is the mother of this child?" By the time she was a month old, my question was not whether I'd be a better mother than my own, but whether I could survive motherhood. Now my own mother is off the hook. I have a lot of empathy.

MOTHER: If you think about it, there's no practical reason to have kids. The financial and emotional burden is staggering and they keep you from doing what you want to do. It's a leap of faith.

It seems like when your children are young, you're always longing for the next step. You can't wait for them to grow up. As you get older time just goes by faster and faster. Being a grandmother gives you a chance to be with one child at a time. You get a second chance. I'm finally getting to the point in my life where I feel okay about all the crazy mixed feelings of life. I'm more accepting of the incongruities and imperfections. Women have more personal freedom with their children than they realize. How you behave with your children becomes their definition of "mother." If you have a career outside the home or stay home baking cookies, that is your child's perception of mother. I didn't realize that when my kids were small. I was reading my Dr. Spock and thinking I had to be a certain, prescribed way. There is no one "perfect" way. You can raise a healthy, happy child without a husband or with a career. It's not easy, but certainly not impossible. Options never occurred to me when I had my babies. The husband had a job and the wife took care of the house and children. I just went blindly along, doing what my own mother had done before me. We really were a silent generation. Women carry a very heavy burden, making themselves responsible for the happiness of those around them. I felt so guilty for so long about being selfish. I had impossible goals of selflessness for myself.

At forty I started my own business with no education or experience to back it up. I just had a gut feeling about my ability to own a clothing shop. My work has given me a whole new outlet to express myself. For the first time, I had to work outside the home. My children knew I had to do it and were supportive. There are a lot of lousy mothers out there and they've spent every waking moment being one. Being there is not a definition of a good mother.

I think one of the most important ingredients for being successful at raising children is feeling good about yourself. I used to think that was wrong, selfish, but now I think selfishness is not a bad thing. It means you'll survive, and enables you to be a happy person and inspire happiness in others.

I left China was I was twenty-seven to come to the United States to marry my husband. The only English word I knew was "Washington." I was just like a piece of furniture, shipped across the world. My own mother was in Red China, so I was separated from my own family before I even left China. My oldest child was born a year later on Lincoln's Birthday, so that's his middle name. I was so happy my first child was a boy because it so pleased my husband. He gave me and the two children nice American names. They were short ones so I could pronounce them. I didn't speak such good English but the television helped my children learn it before they started school. Now they've forgotten their Chinese and they wish I made them speak it more, but I needed to practice my English. I always encouraged them to speak English so they would not fall behind in school.

I now have a son who is a lawyer and a daughter with a Ph.D. A good education for our children was the reason we stayed here instead of going back to China. I stayed home with them until they were both in school all day, then I got a job because we needed more money as they got older. It's always been hard for me to speak or write English. Now my children want me to get a good education just like I used to want for them. I never have any trouble with my kids' growing up. They were more like Chinese than American in that they give their mother respect. In many ways I feel my dreams come true because both of my children are well educated with good jobs; but I wish my daughter would get married and have a child herself. My son has given us a beautiful grandson, but now he is separated from the child's mother. Orientals always want grandchildren, especially boys, to carry the family name. I think Americans feel the same way. No matter where you are from, everyone wants their family to live on after them.

It upsets me how old people are often alone in this country. Everyone seems much more alone and independent here than in China. I don't want to live with my children, but I can't help but want to help out with the grandchildren. My daughter is very American in that she is so independent and capable. That's probably why she is still single. I worry sometimes that many American children have too many material comforts. It can make you weak if you are afraid of hard work. I'm opposed to divorce, but it is hard to keep a family going if both the mother and father work out of the house so much. How can a family sustain itself if no one has time to cook the food or take care of the children? If the man is at work and the woman is at work and the child is at daycare, where is the family? You can't assume your children know you love them. You have to show them.

When I was a little girl, I used to pretend that I lived in the past. Growing up in the South in the 1930s, there was still a lot of bitterness about the Civil War. I always felt it must have been so romantic to live in the days of hoopskirts and lamplight. The Depression was more than an economic condition, it was a state of mind. Sometimes I wished I was a boy, because being an only child, I'm sure I would have been able to follow my father's footsteps into the family business. Since I was female, my dream was to marry someone who ran his own company. Even though women didn't own companies, our family had a strong matriarchal tradition. I never felt like a second-class citizen because I was a girl.

We were such a complacent generation. It never occurred to us to try and rock the system. We were born during the Depression and our husbands were home from World War II, but we didn't openly confront or discuss our problems. It would have been unusual—unthinkable, really—for a housewife in the upper middle class during the 1950s to have a job outside of the house. My own parents would have been horrified. It never

occurred to me or my friends to have a career or try and make a mark on the world. Our children were our only bid to immortality. It never entered my mind to not have children. That was what one did after marriage, like acquiring a house and furniture. There was no such thing as "quality time." Your kids were just part of your everyday life. I'm sure I never had a philosophical discussion about "parenting" with other mothers. When I think back on that period in my life, it seems more remote than my own childhood. The complacency of my life then seems unbelievable to me now.

I was barely twenty-one when I had my first child and it never occurred to me that I wouldn't or couldn't get pregnant. If I had been unable to carry a child, I doubt that I would have adopted because it was very important to me that they be a part of me. I like the feeling of leaving a part of myself behind. To this day I'm not that crazy about babies. Until they are capable of carrying on a conversation, I'm not sure what to do with them. My main motivation for having kids was probably because it was expected of me. It was simply part of living. I don't think I would have had any interest in raising someone else's child.

I think watching your children grow up can help you grow too. They can teach us to sometimes change our own expectations. Raising three teenagers during the sixties and seventies was a wild and curious time. The world was a completely different place from when I was growing up. Being recently divorced and still fairly young myself, I was more willing to look and watch than I probably would have been if I had been locked into a little slot of complacency in middle age and an established marriage. But even during that turbulent era of the late sixties, I never lost faith in the value of good manners and common decency. I think they are the most important things you can teach your children. Manners can indeed make the world a better place. There's no way to avoid coping with others and etiquette gives you tools to get along. Someone said it better than me: "Do unto others as you'd have them do unto you." A sense of place and who you are can carry you through some rough times. Knowing what's expected of you can be a helpful strength.

Even though I thought I would like to teach after I graduated from college, I didn't work when I got married. I stayed home and raised three children. When they were all in grade school, I got a job teaching French and I was one of the first women in our crowd to take a job. Some of my friends were really just shocked that I was going to go work, even though my youngest was in second grade. Teaching was the most convenient profession if you had kids, because you worked mostly when school was in session.

Neighborhoods back in the 1950s were a lot closer knit than today. The women stayed at home, and the parents and children all socialized together. So many nights, all the adults would be together having cocktails while the children played out in the yard. There were no locked doors and not many secrets. It seems like the world was a safer place for raising children back then. We never worried about all those horrible things like kidnapping or child molestation. It never entered our minds to be fearful. I used to always leave my kids in the car when I'd run in for an errand, but I'd be too nervous in today's world to leave my grandchildren in the car while I shopped. There weren't as many strangers in your community as there are today. There were no fences in our yards.

When I was unable to conceive, I never hesitated to adopt a child. We adopted three children and tried to adopt a fourth, but the adoption agency told me I was entirely too selfish. Almost anyone can have children. It's loving them and caring for them that's the most rewarding challenge. An adopted child is very special in that they are never an "accident." They are very wanted children. The joys and problems of raising children are probably the same for adoptive and biological mothers. I didn't have to learn to love my children. I had love at first sight. I almost feel like I loved them before I saw them. You don't have to be pregnant yourself to have a strong nurturing drive. My heart immediately went out to my little babies.

The most difficult challenge of mothering, like any job of responsibility, is making the right decision and being consistent. I feel as responsible for my grown children's happiness now as I did when they were babies. For me, that emotional burden doesn't lighten at all.

The worst fear of every mother is burying a child. It seems out of sync with the laws of nature. After my oldest son died, I was overcome with guilt. He was killed when he was twenty-four. Even though he was a thousand miles away, I felt like I should have been able to protect him somehow. That took a long time to get over. After a time you realize that that type of misery is a form of selfishness, and it's time to go on and stop feeling sorry for yourself. Having two other children helped me go on and rise to the occasion. Through the blame and the pain I gained a lot of insight into how little control we ultimately have in our lives. The church was a great source of strength. I also became more grateful for the support of my friends and relatives. I feel lucky every morning when I wake up and I feel even more thankful for my two living children. I think we make our own heaven or hell here on earth.

When I was a young nurse, I was in charge of sixty babies in the nursery. I felt like a mother even before I had children of my own. Before I was married, my husband and I decided we would have four children. My first son was born prematurely. It was a terrible experience. I'll never forget seeing him so tiny and helpless in the premature nursery. My heart leaped out to him. I don't know how mothers stand losing a child. I think I fell in love with each of my children the first time I felt them flutter inside me. I had to stay in the hospital for ten days and wasn't even allowed to see him or hold him. It was so cruel to keep me separated from him. You can't imagine the frustration, that empty feeling. I finally took the baby home against doctor's orders. He never started to gain weight until I got him out of the hospital.

Being a child of the Depression years, I think I always wanted to give my children all the things we never could afford growing up. I raised my kids during three wars. Since my husband was a career military officer, all the day-to-day responsibilities of child care fell on my shoulders. He was sometimes gone for a year at a time. Of course, the world was a friendlier place then. In a way, life was simpler when we were less affluent. We didn't have to cope with so many things. Television advertising makes kids greedy. It gives them a feeling of emptiness, of wanting things. I don't think that kind of greed makes happy children.

Living with my daughter and her four children gives me a perspective on two generations. I know I'm really an important part of the household. Sometimes my responsibilities become a burden, but mostly I love being needed. When I look at my grandchildren, I think, "What could be more wonderful than this?" Their love is more valuable to me than a clean house.

I really worry about the kind of world my grandchildren are growing up in. I know I can contribute to the quality of my grandchildren's lives by cooking their meals. I'm there for them when they need affection. They love to hear about the past. It's a wonderful gift to give your family a sense of history, of their family roots. After three sons, I was so thrilled when my daughter was born. I think it was one of the happiest days of my life. Now here I am, thirty-two years later, helping her raise her four children. Living together seems logical. She needs my help and I'm glad to give it. I don't think any woman is more blessed with her family than I. An old Greek woman told me, "God gave you everything."

I always had to work. We needed the money. After my first baby was born, I went back to work and my own mother took care of her. I lived in with a family, taking care of their kids. Sometimes I'd leave late at night and come back early in the morning, just so I could get a little peek at my own kids. My husband lived in with me and we'd go visit my momma on our day off. You could make more money as a live-in in Virginia than North Carolina, so I worked in Virginia while my mother raised my kids in North Carolina. I haven't had too many jobs. I lived with one family about seven years and another about eight years. During that time I had two more babies that I left with their grandmamma in North Carolina. The two older ones got used to living there and continued to stay with their grandmamma even after we got a place of our own. They used to hide from me when I'd come visit because they thought I was going to take them away from their grandmother. It didn't bother me, because I knew it meant they were happy where they were. I sent them money every week. After a while though, I wanted to start keeping my own house. I enjoyed live-in work, but I just got tired. I did the cooking, the cleaning, washed and ironed, and watched the children. I knew what needed to be done and just went ahead and did it. I had an intercom in my bedroom at night, and when their parents were out, the kids would come to me. I loved them and they loved me. Life is funny, but it's sweet. I like to remember those times, even though I came to the point where I wanted to have my own place.

I always worked around people who had a lot more things than I did, but I haven't ever envied nobody for nothing. I could see that rich people weren't any happier than I was. No matter what you have, you'll be wantin' something else. I feel like I've basically gotten anything I wanted. If stuff gets too high, I just won't mess with it. I can do without if I have to. I feel like I've been lucky in my life.

I was twenty-nine when I got married in 1938. I continued working through my husband's internship as a doctor and while he was off in World War II. I worked thirteen years until he went into private practice. I was nearly forty when I had my first child. I had several miscarriages before that. Then I had two more girls soon after that. I had three children under three. It was hard on me but good for them. They are still very close. Even though I was a good fifteen years older than my children's friends' parents, I wasn't too aware of it. Having small children kept me young. The world was simpler thirty years ago. It was easier for children to have a childhood.

I really wanted to nurse my babies, but the nurses in the hospital were discouraging and told me I'd never be able to do it. I found out later they were feeding the children in the nursery. I tried awful hard but they just weren't hungry.

When we had babies in the late forties, early fifties, they kept us in the hospital at least ten days. I'll never forget how my oldest daughter had forgotten me when I got home. I had tremendous confidence in my doctors, though. It never occurred to me to question their authority. They figured I was too old to give birth, so I was given a cesarean before I went into labor. Afterward, I did feel cheated, like I had missed out on something. I couldn't believe I'd had a baby. Then they said the next two had to be delivered by cesarean as well. Maybe they should just put a zipper in our bellies.

My daughters today are much more knowledgeable about pregnancy and child care than we were thirty years ago. They read and question more. Watching them grow up has been one of my greatest pleasures and the responsibility of raising them has been my most difficult challenge. Women have more options now. It used to be a tragedy for a woman not to have children. Think of poor Sarah in the Bible. Even the term "barren" is so negative. I think attitudes are much more accepting of childless women now that the working world is more open to women. Also, birth control gives women a choice about motherhood.

I was only fourteen years old when I had my first child. We went ahead and got married and struggled along. I worked in a laundry and my husband had steady work. I scrubbed floors, did anything I had to do, to raise my children. After the third child we had enough money to put down for this house. Somehow it seems like the Lord always provided for us. We eventually had five children together.

My life has always been dedicated to Jesus. My own mother raised her kids in the Church and so did I. I now hold services in my own home every Sunday morning. My favorite hymn as a child was "Stand Up for Jesus," and till this day I'm still standin' up for the Lord. I'm still growing from the strong roots that my mother gave me. She watched my children while I went to work and now I watch eight of my grandchildren while my daughters work. I kept groceries on my momma's table and now my daughter does the same for me. The Lord gives me strength to care for all my little grandchildren. Sometimes I feel like I could turn over mountains. Serving those eight little children supper, when they come round me like little bees, I feel like I'm somebody. Serving my family is one of the ways I serve God. I don't have a great big church to preside over, but that gives me more time for my own family and to go out into the community and help those who need it.

My faith in God has helped me keep this family together. One of my little grandchildren left the fold and had become lost in his ways. He'd been missing for over eight years. I got down on my knees and the tears began to roll. I said, "Lord, send him home to me." Sure enough, he was at my door the next day. God's miracles make anything possible. My own personal happiness comes from the fact that I believe that I'm living God's will. It's no secret what He can do. We enjoy Jesus. My caring doesn't stop with my own kind. I reach out to all of God's family. Black and white, they're all alike. I love them all the same. Sometimes my house is full to overflowed, but that's all right. I never have any trouble sleepin'. I've taught my children, if you see a blind person at the corner, don't you laugh. You go over and help them across the street. I prayed to the Lord to make me a real mother. Just to born a child does not make you a mother. It's taking the responsibility of raisin' that child that really counts. It takes a lot of backbone to raise a child. God can't use a crybaby. The only way to get the strength to do your best is to go before Jesus Christ. I know that I don't have a lot, but I can give my love.

I was eighteen when I first married and twenty when my oldest daughter was born. Now she's sixty-five and I'm eighty-five. She can't deny her age because I don't lie about mine. I raised five children and lost two. One little girl was eight when she was taken down with the diphtheria. I lost my little baby boy in the 1917 flu epidemic when he was only twenty-two hours old. I could feel his little feet turn cold, and he died in my arms. I watched out my bedroom window when they buried him. I went back to bed and laid down and it was seven weeks before I knowed anything. My mother sat by me day and night for seven weeks. When I got out of bed, I was just a shadow. I weighed sixty pounds. The doctor gave me up for dead, but Momma told my husband, "You go and get me some whiskey." He got a gallon of moonshine, and Momma took Turkish towels and kept me wrapped in hot whiskey and broke the pneumonia on me. It was a terrible flu. I believe I got so sick because I'd lost my baby. My heart was broken. Back then we shrouded the dead. We laid the baby out in our trunk until we could get him buried. My oldest child weren't but two years old when the baby died, but for a long time after that she'd go to that trunk and say, "My bubba gone." To this day she swears she can remember that. I can still remember things that happened to me when I was four years old, when my grandma died in 1901. They shrouded her and laid her out on boards and put her in the shed to keep her cool. It was raining

and the roof leaked. They hoisted three umbrellas over my grandmother's body. Momma kept telling me not to go there, but I kept peekin' in, waitin' for her to get up. I can still remember them umbrellas over my grandmother's body.

I stayed at home to raise my babies when they was little. Sometimes I cleaned other people's houses for ten cents an hour. When my children was babies, I didn't have none of that equipment like they have nowadays. The babies just stayed in the bed with me. One time I was raisin' a baby lamb by hand, and that thing got up on the bed with the baby while I was hanging the wash. She was jumpin' right over him, but she never did touch him with her hoofs. I always loved babies, even as a little girl. As a married woman, I always kept my baby doll in the bottom of my trunk, but I lost it when my house burned down seven years ago. I lost everything I ever owned. What hurt me most was to lose all my family pictures. I have loved little children all my life, and I believe that's the reason the good Lord lets me live so long. The Bible says, "Come unto me little children, and thou shalt not suffer." I have never been around a child who didn't love me. I don't believe in beatin' a child. Talk to them. That's how you get 'em to understand. I reckon I spoilt my children, but I can't help it. That's just the way I am. I never did like to spank 'em. I raised five children and nary a one of 'em been in no serious trouble. The three boys went into the army, and the two girls is married and got homes of their own. I think a girl should get married and stay at home to take care of

things. I'm eighty-five years old, and I've kept house all my life. You gotta keep a good reputation. It's something, like your faith, that no one can take away from you.

I got married when I was fifteen, but I'd knowed him long before. I got me a man who didn't drink. He built the house we live in and gave me many children. I thought when I got married, life would be a little easier. But I just jumped out of the frying pan and into the fire. I figured with all the work I was doing raisin' my mama's children they might as well be mine, so I got married and didn't lose no time. I had seven children in ten years. Lord, I had to work like a horse. Drag wood and haul water for a mile. I made the garden, fed the hogs and chickens, plus tended to the children. When my oldest was twelve years old, I went to work in the orchards. I loved staying at home but we needed the money, so off I went. God has been good to me—I didn't lose any of my babies. He's answered my prayers. When we had our fiftieth wedding anniversary, all my children but one was gathered all around and it messed me up. I couldn't enjoy it wondering where the one was at. I'd like to see my sixtieth anniversary with all of my children with us. My oldest is fifty-three and the youngest is forty-three. I have eighteen grandchildren and nine great-grandchildren.

The best time in my life was when my children was little because I could put them to bed and know where they were. I worry about my fifty-three-year-old more now than I ever did when he was little. My husband says they're on their own now. I'll be doggoned if I can say that myself. Sometimes when I think back on how hard I worked when my children were young, I wonder how I stood it. All day on my feet picking apples for a dollar fifty a day, and then walk back with the firewood, fix supper, and milk two cows.

Our kids come by right often—they always call. It's hard enough gettin' along in this world. You do the best you can. Ain't never had nothing handed to me on a silver platter. I've had some good and I've had some bad. That's life. I never had no store-bought diapers. I made my own outta cotton and washed 'em on a board in a tub. Had to carry water from down at the bottom of the hill to wash 'em with, too. I had to miss a day a week to do the wash. It was a three-mile walk. It doesn't make much difference what ya got, it's where your heart is that counts in this life.